THE
PROBLEM
WITH
PAUL

Brian J. Dodd

IVP Academic

An imprint of InterVarsity Press
Downers Grove, Illinois

InterVarsity Press
P.O. Box 1400, Downers Grove, IL 60515-1426
World Wide Web: www.ivpress.com
E-mail: email@ivpress.com

InterVarsity Press®️ is the book-publishing division of InterVarsity Christian Fellowship/USA®️, a student movement active on campus at hundreds of universities, colleges and schools of nursing in the United States of America, and a member movement of the International Fellowship of Evangelical Students. For information about local and regional activities, write Public Relations Dept., InterVarsity Christian Fellowship/USA, 6400 Schroeder Rd., P.O. Box 7895, Madison, WI 53707-7895, or visit the IVCF website at <www.intervarsity.org>.

ISBN 978-0-8308-1871-6

Printed in the United States of America ∞

Library of Congress Cataloging-in-Publication Data

Dodd, Brian J. 1960-
    The problem with Paul/Brian J. Dodd.
        p. cm.
    Includes bibliographical references.
    ISBN 0-8308-1871-5 (paper: alk. paper)
        1. Bible. N.T. Epistles of Paul—Criticism, interpretation, etc.
2. Paul, the Apostle, Saint.   3. Sociology, Biblical.   I. Title.
BS26502.D63   1995
225.9'2—dc20
                                                                    96-4164
                                                                    CIP

P	23	22	21	20	19	18	17	16	15	14	13	12	11	10	9	8
Y	22	21	20	19	18	17	16	15	14	13	12	11	10	09	08	

To Ingrid,
Joel and the
John Wesley Fellows

1

The Problem with Paul

---

*M*any people have problems with the apostle Paul—Christians and non-Christians alike. Depending on views and beliefs, different aspects of Paul's letters jump out at them. Dudley Moore and Peter Cook explain it in a humorous fashion:

PETE: St. Paul's got a . . . lot to answer for.

DUD: He started it, didn't he—all those letters he wrote.

PETE: To the Ephiscans.

DUD: You know, "Dear Ephiscans, Stop enjoying yourself, God's about the place. Signed Paul."

PETE: You can just imagine it, can't you. There's a nice Ephiscan family settling down to a good breakfast of fried mussels and hot coffee and just sitting there. It's a lovely day outside and they're thinking of taking the children out for a picnic by the sea and everything's happy and the sun's coming through the trees, birds are chirping away.

DUD: The distant cry of happy children, and clouds scudding across the sky.

PETE: In fact an idyllic scene is what you'd call it, an idyllic scene. When suddenly into the midst of it all—tap, tap, on the . . . door. You know who it is?

DUD: No.

PETE: It's a messenger bearing a letter from Paul.

DUD: Dad runs to the door to open it, thinking it may be good news.

PETE: Perhaps Grandfather's died and left them the vineyards.

DUD: They open it up and what do they discover?

PETE: "Dear George and Deidre and Family, Stop having a good time, resign yourself to not having a picnic, cover yourself with ashes and start flaying yourselves, until further notice, Signed Paul."

DUD: A dreadful sort of letter to get, isn't it?

PETE: Terrible.[1]

Even though we know that this caricature reflects not a single statement in Paul's letters, still we have to acknowledge that Dud and Pete have captured the reputation Paul has with many people today.

Recently I had opportunity to discuss Paul with a flight attendant on a trans-Atlantic flight. As she made her continual trips up and down the Boeing 767, we discussed what she thought of Paul's view of women and if she found anything redeemable in his writings. Her conclusion was, "He had many things to say for people in his day, and some people today still find value in his writings. But he cannot be modernized. He had no respect for women." In some ways, she is an articulate spokesperson for the modern boycott of the Bible. Although one random conversation is no scientific sample, few would dispute that this bright airline employee speaks for millions of people.

What is surprising is the number of "Bible believers" who have strong reservations about Paul. Having spent a decade leading studies on Paul in churches, I have heard at least one person in every class raise strong reservations about Paul's "male chauvinism," his "arrogance" or his "irresponsible" social views. These critics are not a homogeneous group: a middle-aged attorney, a seventy-year-old retired school teacher, a first-year university student. Furthermore, a number of clergy use some of Paul's "acceptable" lines in their prayers and liturgy but avoid preaching on Paul's letters in favor of the Gospels or the Old Testament prophets.[2] An American bishop recently told me about a fellow bishop who proudly retired without ever having preached a single sermon from the writings of "that Paul."

"There has probably seldom been anyone at the same time hated with such fiery hatred and loved with such strong passion as Paul." With these words Adolf Deissmann describes a paradox that will be explored in this book. For nearly two thousand years Paul has been a pillar of the Christian tradition, yet now he is a problem for many modern readers. For many, Paul says entirely too many objectionable things about women, especially about their relationship to the church and to their husbands. Furthermore, Paul appears virtually indifferent to the issue of slavery, a condition that controlled the lives and children of at least one-third of the population in Rome, Antioch and Alexandria, the urban centers of his day. [3] Indicting Paul for his "sexism" and his silence on the evils of slavery, many modern readers find these reason enough to dismiss Paul.[4]

Why Join the Conversation in This Book

If the test of time proves anything, Paul will not simply fade away. His writings persist, and many people esteem Paul. Why does Paul continue to be held in such high regard? Why have some of the greatest minds of history felt compelled to discuss him? Why do presidents and prime ministers quote him and critics condemn him? If his writings are so remiss, why do such brilliant people honor his name and cite his words? Why do so many scholars spend valuable time putting Paul in his place? If there is any truth to the old adage "Where there is smoke there is fire," then the thoughtful intellectual today must inquire of the smoke surrounding Paul.

The pages that follow are a search, a seeking of the flame at the center of that smoke. At the same time, they must be a conversation, a dialogue with Paul from a modern viewpoint. They are not a defense of Paul. As we will see, he needs no troubadour. Rather, they are a conversation with this rabbi-turned-Christian-missionary, addressing today's concerns to his ancient presentation of himself and his ideas.[5]

The contemporary critic of Paul may be morally obligated to eavesdrop on this conversation. Paul's persistence and influence on the modern world demand a thinking person's attention. George Bernard Shaw once said, "It was Paul who converted the religion that has raised one man above sin and death into a religion that delivered millions of men so completely into a dominion that their own common nature became a horror to them, and the religious life became a denial of life."[6] If Paul really is responsible for such a violation of human dignity, then conscience demands that we unlock the bars of Paul's message and free those held captive from his tyranny—that is, if Shaw is right.

Those completely committed to Paul's message may want to overhear these words too. Though the persistence of Paul's teachings for almost two thousand years is enough for some pragmatists to ignore Paul's current critics, there is reason to hear the other side of the conversation—the compelling criticisms of contemporary people of conscience. If for no other reason, Christians must ponder the problem Paul's critics create for Christian witness. Though Paul's name graces many churches, some of those same churches are experiencing a boycott every Sunday by people who are not merely "sleeping in" as the pulpit pundits sometimes suggest. The apostle Paul's church may need to know the problem their namesake creates for their outreach. Paul may be a pillar of Christian theology, but he is also sometimes a problem for Christian mission.

This book is an invitation to several parties to join this conversation:

1. seekers who want answers to their reservations about this part of the Bible;

2. Christians for whom Paul's letters are sacred text (an unthinking dismissal of Paul's teaching on certain issues creates a casual attitude toward the Bible generally, and such a jaundiced outlook needs to be carefully considered);

3. serious Bible students who want to (a) deepen their understanding of the social context of Paul's letters and (b) hone their critical awareness of the demands of interpreting and applying this ancient and sacred text to our sometimes quite different social situation.

This book is meant to open up a conversation between several parties, but this is not always our natural inclination. Our normal engagement with books and articles is individualistic. If the line in the diagram below represents our "conversation" with a text or its author, the common pattern of reading appears something like this:

me ————▶ Paul

There is nothing wrong with this approach to a text, but I point it out because this habit dramatically affects how we read an ancient text such as the Bible. Too many people naively suppose that, since the Bible has been translated into their native language, interpreting it is simply a matter of reading it. Of course, Christians believe that God's Spirit supervises this process and gives us the ability to grasp what God wants us to understand (Jn 16:13). Thus, the diagram above and those below need to be understood to have an Invisible Conversation Partner, who guides and enables our reading and gives us renewed minds for the task (see Rom 12:2).

Although it is true that much value can be received from the Bible in an individualistic approach, good interpretation of Paul's letters requires a realization that we are hearing just one-half of an original conversation between Paul (text) and his original hearers:

Paul ————▶ original readers

When we read Paul's first letter to the Corinthians, for example, it is obvious that we join the conversation in the middle: "It has been reported to me by Chloe's people that there are quarrels among you" (1 Cor 1:11), and "Now concerning the matters about which you wrote . . ." (1 Cor 7:1). Paul did not write with you and me in mind, nor did he realize that he was writing chapters for the Bible. If he had, surely he would have explained many things that he left unsaid because he already knew what his original readers knew. In the case of 1 Corinthians, he wrote about concrete issues to newly converted Christians in the southern part of Greece in the middle of the first century.

For us fully to appreciate Paul's letters, we have to do two things at once: We have to study Paul's letters to see what they are saying in their original, ancient context, and we have to attempt to understand the other end of the conversation from his readers' point of view. The second part of this project takes effort and requires humility. Sometimes we simply do not know what conversation was being had and what issues were at stake. A better diagram of good interpretation should look something like this:

me ————▶ Paul ————▶ original readers

We do not have access to the original readers, but we attempt to make sense of the conversation Paul was having with them. Much of the time, fortunately, Paul says enough for us to understand what is going on. It is similar to the experience of overhearing someone talking on the phone. Although we hear only half of the conversation, often we are able to piece together much of the whole. Sometimes, however, we are mistaken, and we miss many of the nuances that the two on the phone are privy to.

But there is another conversation partner required for understanding the Bible. Individualistic interpretation of ancient texts such as the Bible overlooks this. All English readers of the Bible are dependent on another conversation, whether they realize it or not:

me ————▶ other readers ————▶ Paul

These "other readers" are, at a minimum, scholars who read Hebrew or Greek and who have translated the Bible into our language. Translation itself is an art, not a science. Translators see their work as a process that requires them to keep an ongoing conversation with other scholars because more is continually learned about the ancient languages and because our own language is constantly changing.

For Christians, these "other readers" should be a valued part of interpretation. After all, not only are individual Christians given the Spirit to lead them into understanding God's ways, the Christian community is given specially gifted people to teach and interpret God's ways "for the common good" of all (1 Cor 12:3-11, 27-31). Because Christians are member-parts of the "body of Christ," each one's gifts need to be valued, respected and utilized. Truly then, an individualistic approach to understanding the ancient text of the Bible, although better than nothing, is not as good *or as biblical* as a team effort.

The best way to understand the Bible, then, is to engage in a four-way conversation between ourselves, other readers, Paul and his original readers (five-way, when we factor in the help given by God's Spirit). In this process we have to assume a posture of humility and be open to realizing that sometimes what we thought Paul meant is not what he meant at all. There is, therefore, a better diagram that incorporates this fourth group of conversation partners:

me ———▶ other readers ————▶ Paul ————▶ original readers

We can engage this fourth group of "other readers" in several ways: by interacting with Bible commentaries and studies such as this one; by using a Bible with study notes; by talking with other readers of the Bible—whether they have more training or not (out of the mouth of babes!); and by making use of a key resource found in nearly every community. This key resource is the many gifted and equipped pastors. Most of them are highly trained in understanding the Bible, and I have never met one who is not eager to help untangle a knotty passage. Any reader who finds the conversation in this book confusing will likely find in a local pastor an able and wise help.

In this book I expand the circle of "other readers" to include those who are critical of Paul. Many people, Christian and non-Christian alike, who have negative appraisals of Paul's letters, base their judgments on an individualistic approach. Many others raise compelling criticisms that need to be addressed. These critical readers sometimes have little regard for tradition or history or the Bible as forms of authority; consequently they raise questions that others may never consider. They may have never conversed with Bible scholars, and Bible believers may have never seriously listened to their (often well-reasoned) reservations about the Bible.

When someone proclaims Paul's ideas in a monologue, without pausing to hear other views, intelligent critics often quietly hang up the phone. On the other hand, these critics often try Paul in a contemporary court, neglecting his rights as an ancient person, granting him no competent counsel. Their (mis)understanding of Paul has been used to try, convict and condemn him to the prison of indifference. Dud and Pete's misrepresented Paul never existed, but the historical Paul often pays the penalty for a mythic misrepresentation of his words and deeds.

What follows is a conversation with Paul and his readers, ancient and modern. To read on is to agree to listen and enter into this conversation. But would Paul have cared to join in? To present him as a conversationalist already misrepresents him if the assumption is that he did not value the views of people who thought differently. The question of Paul's attitude toward dialogue requires two answers that must be held together.

On the one hand, Paul silenced dissidents. To be sure, he let some speak, but he seemed comfortable muzzling others and removing them from the conversation, usually because he believed that the eternal destiny of his followers was at stake. For example, Paul was not open to discussing the issue of the man who slept with his stepmother (1 Cor 5). He pronounced, in effect, "Kick him out of the church." Elsewhere he condemned to hell those with a more Jewish understanding of Christianity who were telling his followers in Galatia that they must also have their foreskins trimmed (Gal 1:8-9). Sarcastically he wished—out loud!—that the knife would slip and cut the whole thing off (Gal 5:12). Clearly, Paul did not allow anyone and everyone to come to the discussion table.

On the other hand, Paul did allow many people into the conversation. I suggest the following as examples of Paul as a conversationalist who would want to engage in the dialogue of the following chapters:

1. Paul wrote in Greek, the *lingua franca* of his day. It may be that he had to. Yet he wrote to be understood, using illustrations, analogies and repetition to make clear his views. Moreover, he drew many of his theological images from concrete social situations. For example, he portrays salvation in his letter to the Romans both as "redemption," an image of the freed slave, and as "justification," an image from the courts. Furthermore, he wrote in the fashion of other typical Greek letters, though he does many creative and unique things with the form. He clearly wanted to be understood by his Greco-Roman conversation partners.

2. He wrote in response to the ideas, actions and questions of others. He dialogued with them. Chloe's people brought a report to Paul of troubles in

Corinth, and he wrote in reply to the issues they raised (see 1 Cor 1:11; 7:1; 8:1). In his letter to the Romans, Paul used a discussion-style of writing, known in scholarly circles as "diatribe." Not to be confused with the popular use of the term today as a bitter verbal attack, a diatribe was an ancient, interactive style wherein the speaker or writer engaged opposing views, real and hypothetical, and argued a case against their objections.[7] In fact, Paul demonstrates by his use of the diatribe style in Romans that he is happy with a conversational approach.

3. He identified with the feelings and experiences of his readers. For example, in 1 Thessalonians 1:6-10 Paul makes clear to the Thessalonians that he understands from experience what it is like to suffer persecution as a promoter of the Christian gospel. In Philemon he identifies with the experience of the slave Onesimus and appeals on his behalf.

4. Paul shared his work and trusted others with the task of communicating with his churches. He claimed a huge number of coworkers—more than a hundred are listed in his letters.[8] They assisted him in writing his letters and interpreted them to the churches.[9] There is no evidence that they were his slaves, and he disavows having any personal charisma, so why their loyalty to "that Paul"? Why did they risk the dangers of ancient travel and stand by his side against belligerent hostility? Consider uncircumcised Titus's willingness to be a test case in Jerusalem in Galatians 2. This, no doubt, is a tribute both to his courage and to his loyalty to Paul. It is likely that Paul showed the consideration and mutual concern necessary for a leader to command this kind of extraordinary trust and loyalty.

5. Luke reports in Acts 17 that Paul conversed both in the synagogue and in the marketplace. Paul stood among the philosophers of the day in the Areopagus, affirmed the religiosity of the Athenians and began his debate by appealing to the inscription on one of their idols, "To an unknown god." In this same incident he merely alludes to the Hebrew Scriptures, which were his mother's milk, but he actually cites Aratus and perhaps Epimenides, two Greek poets. Luke, who claims to have known Paul, paints a picture of him as a man who willingly entered dialogue with those of far different viewpoints.

6. Paul actually cites cutting remarks made about him and gives them his

energy and attention. For example, in 2 Corinthians 10:10 he writes, "For they say, 'His letters are weighty and strong, but his bodily presence is weak, and his speech contemptible.' " Paul himself records this criticism for posterity.

Surely, then, Paul would dialogue with a contemporary critic, if he only could. So let the conversation begin.

2

The Male Chauvinist & the Modern Woman

---

*O*ne of the most memorable vacations of my childhood was a family expedition from the hot California Central Valley to the lush, cool scenery of British Columbia. My older sister and I played captains of the camper from the lookout over the cab of the truck. We were brave. We were bold. There was nothing we couldn't imagine from our perch above the traffic.

When we arrived at the Capilano suspension bridge, our boldness led us forth to conquer the largest pedestrian suspension bridge in the world. The cables and wood spanned 450 feet of a spectacular gorge, and it seemed at least that far to the bottom. It was a scene that is forever etched in my memory because of its grandeur and terror.

My sister led the way forward, but when I realized the magnitude of the situation, my confidence failed me. Though born from the same genetic pool, my sister inherited none of the fear of heights that plagued me at that moment.

She leaped confidently onto the gently swaying bridge while I crept cautiously, inching my way out as I gripped the handrail. A gentle leader, she coaxed and encouraged me to the center of the bridge. Once there, suspended above the gorge, her kindness fled, and she took sheer delight in shaking the bridge from side to side, encouraged by the echoes of my screams.

The problem of Paul is like that swaying bridge. Paul is on the far side of the chasm in another social world. We are separated from Paul by language, culture and time, holding in our hands his words translated into our own heart language. When we interpret those words, we must cross an interpretive bridge, and as we cross the bridge we take our cultural and linguistic biases with us, seeking to get closer and closer to Paul's original meaning. The bridge is an imaginative construction, a work of self-discipline in which we seek to encounter Paul on his terms and then appropriate his message in our terms. Interpretation involves traveling both ways over the bridge. We go from our lives and situations to Paul's, but then we must work to bring Paul's message back again to us. The bridge of interpretation is a good way to conceive of the problem of Paul for three reasons.

First, it portrays a gap of understanding between us and Paul. True, we share many human experiences in common, but many we do not. On our side is what the text *means* and *implies* for us in our situation. On Paul's side is what the text *meant* and *implied* for the original readers. For us to understand Paul's letters, we must cross the bridge, as much as we can, to understand them in their original setting.

Second, the bridge analogy reminds us that, when we have interpreted Paul's letters on his terms, we must cross the bridge again to apply his message to a different time and place, one that Paul had no awareness of when he composed his letters. We may think that Paul's words are completely relevant or totally reckless, but Paul himself cannot readily help us as we cross over to our side of the bridge. For example, Paul gave instructions to slaves, but that teaching now must be interpreted and applied in a society where slavery has not existed for more than a century, and even the slavery in our recent history often took a much more savage form than that of Paul's day. The allegory of the bridge reminds us of the effort and emotion that interpretation involves, particularly when it comes to applying the message today.

Third, the allegory of the bridge sensitizes us to the feelings of those around us when we consider these issues. The interpretation of the Bible often divides us into the bold, who launch out and make confident statements about the meaning of the Bible, and the cautious, who approach the interpretive journey with trepidation. Take the issue of the ordination of women. Some launch out on the bridge with confidence, claiming that the Bible and the Spirit of God are surely in favor of the full inclusion of women as leaders in the church. For others, it seems as though the bravado of these progressives will tear the bridge from its moorings and crash the church to the ground.

In the pages that follow it may appear that at some points I shake the bridge too hard and, at others, that I cling too tightly to the rails, paralyzed in fear. In any case, this book is meant to be a part of an ongoing conversation where we all have something to learn. In light of the problem of the interpretive bridge, we now turn to the problem presented by Paul's views on women.

Is Paul a Sexist?

Is Paul a sexist? The question itself is hopelessly blind to the problem of the bridge. Should the question read "*Is* Paul a sexist?" or "*Was* Paul a sexist?" If we ask it the first way, we decide to ignore the bridge and the chasm and pretend that Paul somehow lives on our side of the gorge. Sexism is a phenomenon that only recently has been given a label with a simple, indisputable identifier: making distinctions of rights, privileges and duties based on gender identification. Clearly, Paul makes such distinctions: women are to pray with their heads covered (1 Cor 11:2-16), to be silent in church (1 Cor 14:34-35) and not to exercise teaching authority over men (1 Tim 2:11-15).[1] So it is tempting to make an equally clear claim: "Paul *is* a sexist."

But another issue must be factored in. Paul is dead—and has been for some two millennia. To say "Paul *is* a sexist" ignores this basic fact. Okay, so we change the claim to "Paul *was* a sexist." But now another problem confronts us. Though the popular *Back to the Future* movie series suggests otherwise, when we go back to Paul's time, we lose our contemporary consciousness as we travel. When we land on the shores of Greco-Roman civilization, we no longer have our English language, our democratic sensibilities, our labels and our contemporary "isms." We arrive in Corinth or Ephesus only by the force of imagination and reconstruction, and at best we can only observe and make note of what happened and what was said. Stripped of our heightened sensitivity about women's dignity, would we recognize Paul as a sexist?

Those who dare to answer yes have to confront the force of historical precedent: Who before the modern age thought so? Our perceptions of Paul are tied up with where we stand in history and culture. (The discussion here may not even be comprehensible in contemporary male-dominated societies around the globe!) To believe that we would have lived and spoken differently is a fiction, since we have never walked in the shoes of those ancient actors on the stage of social history. Humility requires us to respect the chasm of time and culture.

Was Paul a Feminist?

An awareness of Paul's cultural setting makes the opposite question far more relevant: Was Paul a feminist? Before answering, we must acknowledge that the word *feminist* did not appear until the end of the nineteenth century.[2] The word *feminist* is as anachronistic as is *sexist*. Yet there is a telling difference between the two revealed in this question: *How would Paul's attitude toward women have been perceived in his day using our anachronistic terms?* It is common today to view Paul as a male chauvinist, a misogynist, a neurotic hater of women. This glib caricature is often repeated in many ways. But before we settle for this assessment, we should give full weight to some observations about the gender sensitivities of Paul's day.

Paul lived in a time when women and children had a far lower status than they do today. The social role of women remained largely that of homemaker and wife, though they could become successful in certain businesses. (Paul's first convert in Philippi, according to Acts 16:11-15, was Lydia, a merchant of purple cloth, who was able to travel from Asia Minor to Macedonia.) Women were largely uneducated and illiterate, as were the vast majority of men in the Roman empire. Some men were educated; most women were not. Men took positions of leadership within the community, whereas women generally stayed in the background. In our terms, Paul's world was sexist and hierarchical.

In light of this, it is not Paul's "sexist" comments that would have struck the women and men of his day but his progressive comments about women. His statements that appear to place women hierarchically beneath men would not have been in any sense unique in a world of slavery and subjugation. But his comments that value women and place them front and center in the community leap off the page. It is worth surveying these positive and somewhat liberal views, since they need to be factored into an assessment of the issue of Paul and women.[3]

The evidence of Romans. If we page through Paul's letters in their New Testament order, the first letter we come to is Romans. Romans, the longest of Paul's letters, was written later than many of his other letters. Here we find the heart of Paul's message—a message that applies equally to women and to men: "There is therefore now no condemnation for those who are in Christ Jesus" (Romans 8:1). If we look for gender specific evidence of Paul's attitude toward women in Romans, the first evidence comes in the greetings of Romans 16. The first leader mentioned is Phoebe, a deacon *(diakonos)* of the church at Cenchrae whom Paul recommends to the Romans, claiming that she has the same right to be supported as do all traveling missionaries (vv. 1-2). Paul uses the same word stem *(diakon-)* for her work in Cenchrae as he does in the defense of his own ministry in 2 Corinthians, and he uses it elsewhere chiefly for those who proclaim the gospel.[4]

Her designation as "deacon" points to her high status among the community, and she is given a recommendation to the church in Rome that equals the recommendation given to Timothy as Paul's representative to Corinth (compare 1 Cor 4:17; 16:10-11). Timothy served as letter carrier for 1 Corinthians, and it is highly likely—though not explicitly stated—that Phoebe was the letter carrier and authoritative interpreter for the Roman Christians as Paul's personal envoy.[5] It is no insignificant claim to fame to have been the carrier and explainer of the letter to the Romans, possibly the most important book of the New Testament.

The nineteenth-century African-American evangelist Julia A. J. Foote said,

"When Paul said, 'Help those women who labor with me in the Gospel' he certainly meant that they did more than pour out tea."[6] Her witty assessment is borne out in the comments Paul makes about other women in Romans 16. In the next verse, Prisca is mentioned with Aquila (v. 3). In a society where women were subjugated, commentators have long recognized how striking it is that Paul mentions Prisca, a woman, before Aquila, a man.

This prominent position might be because of her higher social status or because of her prominence among the early Christian communities as a missionary. The latter reason is more probable since Prisca and Aquila are spoken of together as those "who work with" (are coworkers of) Paul. To the uninitiated, this may seem a benign designation, but the term *coworker (synergos)* is often used throughout Paul's letters as a high-status designation of missionaries with whom he sees himself as a partner. He uses the same term for this woman missionary as he uses for his own missionary service, as well as for the gospel work of Apollos, Timothy, Mark and Luke, to name a few (see Rom 16:9, 21; 1 Cor 3:9; 2 Cor 6:1; 8:23; Phil 2:25; 4:3; Col 4:11; 1 Thess 3:2; Philem 1, 24).[7] Granting Prisca the same authoritative designation as these important dignitaries in the early Christian community implies her importance as a missionary worker. In fact, Acts 18 leaves no doubt that she, along with her husband, took aside the polished and sophisticated Apollos to explain "the Way of God to him more accurately" (v. 26). The fact that Prisca's life was threatened along with Aquila's makes clear she was not simply serving tea while he preached (Rom 16:4).

Most striking is the mention of Andronicus and Junia (Rom 16:7). Again, a woman is included in the missionary circle as a prisoner with Paul (see Col 4:10; Philem 23), and she is identified as one of the most outstanding apostles. Chrysostom, the early church father who was a native Greek speaker, gives us the correct impact of this verse: "Oh! How great is the devotion of this woman, that she should be counted worthy of the appellation of the apostle!"[8] Although some have tried to argue that Junia was really a man named Junias (see NIV), the stronger case is decidedly in favor of the feminine (see NRSV).[9] "Apostle" was used by Paul to refer to a large band of authoritative missionaries among whom Junia and Andronicus had made a name for themselves (compare 1 Cor 15:5-9).[10] We are accustomed to hearing of the life and teaching of "the apostle Paul," sometimes abbreviated as "the Apostle." It is striking that Paul recognizes this highly authoritative status of this woman missionary.

Mary (Rom 16:6) is characterized in missionary language as one who "has worked very hard" and Tryphaena and Tryphosa (v. 12) as "workers in the Lord."[11] All totaled, of the twenty-seven people mentioned by name in Romans 16, nine (one-third) of them are women, and four of these women are spoken of with high esteem because of their missionary efforts.

Phoebe is mentioned before any men because of her role as a letter carrier and interpreter; Prisca is given prominence above her husband; and Junia the apostle bears the most esteemed missionary designation of the early church. The initial impression one must have of Paul is that he highly valued women alongside men in the missionary enterprise to which he had been called.

The witness of 1 Corinthians. The next letter is 1 Corinthians, and the first person mentioned by name is Chloe—a woman (1 Cor 1:11)! This fact is striking since we might first expect to hear the name of a male leader, but beyond this it is difficult to know who she was. Paul simply says that "Chloe's people" had brought him news of the troubles in their church. Perhaps they were her slaves, since it is likely she was a householder who hosted one of the house churches in Corinth. That she was able to send messengers to Paul about the affairs of the church indicates that she was a woman of prominence and power. Paul recognizes her as a person of status and authority in the community.

In 1 Corinthians 5, Paul gives instructions on the harsh discipline of a man in an incestuous relationship with his stepmother. In a "sexist" society, might we not expect Paul to vilify the woman? That is exactly what happened in John 8:3-11 when they brought to Jesus the woman—*but not the man*—caught in adultery. Indeed, that is the common double standard still prevalent in our society: a woman is "promiscuous," but a man "has indiscretions"—both referring to adulterous relationships. In 1 Corinthians 5 Paul focuses on the man apparently because he, not his stepmother, was part of the Christian community—but Paul addresses the man nevertheless.

In 1 Corinthians 7, Paul gives instructions on abstention from sex and on marriage and divorce, subjects to which we shall return. What is of interest here is that in a society that practiced a double standard for men and women regarding sex, marriage and divorce, Paul is at pains to show that men are under the same sex and marriage ethic as women:

The husband should give to his wife her conjugal rights, and likewise the wife to her husband. (v. 3)

The wife does not have authority over her own body, but the husband does; likewise the husband does not have authority over his own body, but the wife does. (v. 4)

The wife should not separate from her husband . . . and . . . the husband should not divorce his wife. (vv. 10-11)

The unbelieving husband is made holy through his wife, and the unbelieving wife is made holy through her husband. (v. 14)

Wife, for all you know, you might save your husband. Husband, for all you know, you might save your wife. (v. 16)

The married man is anxious about the affairs of the world, how to please his wife, and his interests are divided. And the unmarried woman and the virgin are anxious about the affairs of the Lord, so that they may be holy in body and spirit; but the married woman is anxious about the affairs of the world, how to please her husband. (vv. 33-34)

In this last example, it is even more striking that Paul appears to place the status of single women over that of married men and women, a move that must have struck the Corinthians as a radical reversal of the normal social privileges of married men.[12] As one university student said, "Paul sounds like he had attended gender sensitivity training." If we cannot properly call such balance "feminist," we have to acknowledge that Paul would have appeared to his contemporaries to be on that end of the scale. In fact, it may be that Paul's later restrictions on women's behavior were necessary because of the implications his converts were drawing from his very progressive views on such things. When Paul saw how far they were taking his teaching and the effects it was having on those he was seeking to convert, he may have pulled in the reins "for the sake of the gospel" (1 Cor 9:19-23) "so that the word of

God may not be discredited" (Tit 2:5).

First Corinthians 11 is a notoriously problematic chapter, but there are indications of a protofeminist Paul here too. It is clear that Paul believes that women as well as men are granted power to prophesy by God's Spirit (v. 5), though this is in some tension with the also difficult 1 Corinthians 14:33-36.[13] Although it comes amid a chapter that emphasizes the male-female hierarchy in the order of things, Paul strikes an egalitarian balance: "In the Lord woman is not independent of man or man independent of woman. For just as woman came from man, so man comes through woman; but all things come from God" (1 Cor 11:11-12). This seems to be a partial corrective of the impression that Paul is in favor of subjugating women here.[14] Though men and women are to dress differently for worship according to the conventions of their culture, they are mutually interdependent on each other.

The balance of Galatians. The most-quoted passage in defense of Paul's egalitarianism is Galatians 3:26-28. Paul makes clear that all human beings have equal status before God through Christ: "In Christ Jesus you are all children of God through faith. As many of you as were baptized into Christ have clothed yourselves with Christ. There is no longer Jew or Greek, there is no longer slave or free, there is no longer male and female; for all of you are one in Christ Jesus."

This is the high water mark of Paul's attitude about women, slaves and Gentiles (see also 1 Cor 12:13; Col 3:11). Coming from a cultural and religious perspective that saw these groups as inferior, Paul in this passage reflects a spiritual equality that he was eager to work out in his churches. He does not, however, develop a program of political emancipation, which in antiquity would have been unthinkable. (The Romans did not circulate public opinion polls and were ruthless in quashing rebellion.)

Mutuality in Ephesians. Ephesians 5:21-33 is a unit that begins with a command to *mutual* submission: "Be subject to one another out of reverence for Christ." The verb "be subject" *(hypotassō)* does not occur in verse 22, but the grammar makes clear that a wife's subjection to her husband is an example of the general command to all believers in verse 21. What follows in verses 21-33 are two applications of verse 21, wives and husbands submitting to each other in mutual love and respect. This passage cannot be cited to justify a husband's domineering, demeaning or controlling his wife, an interpretation that is clearly a misreading. Paul's teaching is exactly the opposite: mutual submission means that husbands are *not* to domineer their wives but to treat them with the same love and consideration that Christ shows toward the church (vv. 23-33).

The answer of 1 Thessalonians. It has struck more than one interpreter that Paul uses feminine imagery in 1 Thessalonians 2 to depict his use of authority: "We might have made demands as apostles of Christ. But we were gentle among you, like a nurse tenderly caring for her own children" (vv. 6-7). Paul portrays his apostleship in traditionally feminine imagery. This observation may serve to broaden our perception of how Paul viewed women.[15] Also relevant here is Galatians 4:19: "My little children, for whom I am again in the pain of childbirth until Christ is formed in you."[16] In both cases we find that Paul's self-presentation is somewhat maternal.

Conclusion. Paul's attitude toward women clearly includes some progressive notions. Paul fits, even as an ancient man, Mary Stewart van Leeuwen's recent definition of a "Christian feminist": "a person of either sex who sees women and men as equally saved, equally Spirit-filled and equally sent."[17] Paul clearly taught all three: women and men are *equally* saved (Gal 3:28), *equally* gifted (1 Cor 11:4-5) and *equally* sent for gospel labor (Rom 16:1-5).

Indirect evidence to support this impression comes from the history of the expansion and growth of the early church. In his treatment of some causes of the growth of the early church, Oxford professor Henry Chadwick noted that Christianity had a strong appeal among women for three reasons: because Christians believed in the equality of women with men before God; because husbands were taught not to domineer their wives but to treat them with the same love and consideration Christ shows for his church (Eph 5:25-33); and because husbands were under the same sex ethic as their wives, unlike the double standard for men and women found in pagan society.[18]

Although it is true that Paul appears progressive in his context—on his side of the interpretive bridge—some of his exhortations to the women in his day appear to subjugate women and make him look like the archmisogynist from our side of the bridge. So, while keeping in mind the very progressive approach of Paul for his time in the many instances mentioned, we must now address the question, How do we bring Paul's message back to our side of the bridge, where women as well as men presume that they will define their own marital and vocational roles?

How Should We Treat What Paul Said About Women Today?

Most things Paul says about women are positive and need little effort to interpret for today: women are equally saved by Christ, equally gifted by the Spirit and equally sent for mission. Only a few of Paul's statements about women and marriage are controversial and evoke one of three responses: an all-or-nothing reaction; a sophisticated reinterpretation of "what Paul really meant"; or a careful handling of the cultural elements of Paul's letters, interpreting one Scripture in light of what others say.

All-or-nothing approach. The knee-jerk response for many people is to take the simplest approach to many of life's issues, either accepting or rejecting everything as is. The total-acceptance response is naively unaware of the problem of the interpretive bridge, whereas the one who dismisses Paul in his entirety misses out on many treasures of the Bible. While these options are the least complex, neither of them is sufficiently sophisticated. Uncritical acceptance fails to explain the unavoidable: the Bible must and should be interpreted and cannot simply be "read and believed," since *all* reading necessarily entails interpretation. Total rejection reflects an uncritical ability to assess and retrieve the truly valuable and enduring truths embedded in the cultural containers of Paul's letters.

Revision. Another trend is to attempt to revise what Paul said or meant, or to shift the problem to another author. Gerda Lerner enthusiastically states a commonly held assessment of this approach:

> Modern biblical scholarship has reached near-consensus in the judgment that most of the comments pertaining to women attributed to Paul were not in fact written or spoken by Paul but were the product of post-apostolic writers who ascribed the texts to him for greater authority. This includes the admonition most often cited: that women "must learn in silence and

with all submissiveness. I permit no woman to teach or to have authority over men; she is to keep silent" (1 Tim 2:11). Knowledge of this erroneous ascription was, of course, not available to women until the present day, so that for nearly 2000 years the misogynist Paulinist tradition, which has dominated biblical interpretation, was regarded as apostolic.[19]

We must set aside the flagrant falsehood of her opening statement (no such "near-consensus" exists) to examine this style of addressing the cultural elements of Paul's letters. This revisionist approach is simple: Paul was not a sexist like his later interpreters, who have put their "misogynist" words into his mouth. Nineteen centuries of the church were apparently unaware that Paul never said such things, but somehow we now have this critical awareness and so are not to be troubled by 1 Timothy.

This solution is unsatisfactory and unconvincing. First of all, 1 Corinthians 11:2-16 and 14:34-35 are still indisputably Paul's writing,[20] by themselves creating the same problem for women, regardless of what we do with Ephesians and 1 Timothy. Second, 1 Timothy is canonized as Scripture, and those who accept it as Scripture still have to confront the issue of what to do with these words that have been accepted as holy writ. Even were we to agree with those scholars who accept that 1 Timothy is written by a Paulinist rather than by Paul, that does not solve the issue of how we should interpret, apply and enforce the teaching of this letter as part of the canon of Scripture.

Careful interpretation with cultural and contextual sensitivity. Interpretation is a demanding discipline that requires us to interpret the individual parts of Paul's letters in light of the larger context of his writings and then in light of the larger message of the Bible. As we have seen, Paul's approach to women generally is positive. In the first place, we must be sensitive to Paul's social world and assess his comments about women in relation to the hierarchy of his culture, not in relation to the progressiveness of ours. We must travel back across the interpretive bridge to Paul's world to understand him on his own terms, then we must travel back to our day and apply his teaching to our often new situation, relying on the counsel of the entire Bible.

For example, Paul says, "Every woman who prays or prophesies . . . should cover her head" (1 Cor 11:5-6, NIV), but few Western Christians today apply this command the same way the Corinthians were to apply it in their quite different culture. (The veiling Paul prescribes and the fashion statement of a fancy hat are not the same thing.) Why? Paul's teaching relates to an issue of etiquette and propriety in Corinthian sensitivity about women's hair that we do not face in our culture. Praying with uncovered heads in Paul's day would have offended sensibilities, similar to a woman serving communion in a mini-skirt would today.[21] When we travel across the bridge of culture, we realize that Paul lived in a world where a woman's uncovered head was sexually suggestive, the closest parallel for us being skimpy clothing.

Paul is calling for mutual regard in a Corinthian Christian community where people had gone overboard with their liberties. Paul has to remind them of the significance of community regard (1 Cor 6—11) and love (1 Cor 13) as ones who want to celebrate the benefits of the resurrected Christ (1 Cor 15). Though some felt free to cast off their coverings because of their freedom in Christ, Paul reminds the entire community (1 Cor 8—14) that freedom in Christ requires self-limitation of some liberties for the sake of others.

At this point some may object, "Either all of Paul's words apply today exactly as they did in his day, or none of them do. Women should have their heads covered when they pray, keep silent in church and never exercise authority over men." Although we may feel more secure to greet one another with a holy kiss and to make women again wear head-coverings, we take a step backward in our understanding of the Bible if we ignore the clearly culture-specific elements by imposing that culture upon our own. For some of us, the prospect of identifying cultural elements in Paul's letters may feel as though someone is shaking the interpretive suspension bridge, raising feelings of fear or concern. But we must boldly accept a claim that is compatible with valuing the Bible as God's Word: The Bible is the Word of God communicated through the language and culture of humans.

Unlike Muslim claims that the Koran is the direct word of God, Christians have maintained that the Bible is the revelation of God through the words and actions of human beings. In the center of that revelation—Jesus Christ—God reveals himself as a human being, approachable and understandable precisely because he limited himself for a time in human form. In fact, the Christian confession about Christ is exactly paralleled in our highest view of Scripture. As Jesus was fully God and fully human, so the Bible is fully God's Word and completely human literature. There is mystery in this affirmation, but all the greatest truths of the Christian faith are surrounded in mystery, awe and wonder.

To claim that not all of the Bible applies today in a one-to-one correspondence with how it applied to its original hearers is not to deny the blessed divinity of its nature as God's Word but to affirm the obvious human character of its pages. It is fully divine and *fully human*. This is to acknowledge that some of the Bible's assertions should be reapplied to our current human situation. In removing the cultural hull of the text, we should be careful that we do not throw away the divine nut with the human shell. But, if we want any of the nut for our spiritual nourishment, we must critically interpret the time-bound elements. Some (most?) of the Bible needs little such adaptation.

"I say to you, Love your enemies and pray for those who persecute you" (Mt 5:44) is self-standing in any time and in any place, though the ferocity of the persecution encountered varies dramatically. But even texts that are straightforward require us to travel the interpretive bridge. In the case of Matthew 5:44, what we read has been translated from Greek to English, which itself requires some cultural-linguistic interpretation so that we do not end up with a whole different sense, such as "pray for those who *seek after* you," which is also a possible and common translation of the Greek word *diōkō*. This is an example of the many ways in which our English translations of the Bible are indebted to linguistic scholars who take the interpretive bridge seriously.

In the case of women praying with their heads covered, I believe that most of us have it right when we suggest (either explicitly or implicitly by our silence on the matter) that we should not apply this teaching in our culture the same way Paul applied it in his. As Gordon Fee says in his commentary on 1 Corinthians, "The fact that Paul's own argument is so tied to cultural norms suggests that literal obedience is not mandatory for obedience to God's Word."[22] Fee states clearly what so many apply intuitively, but three qualifications should be made.

First, we should seek the *principle* that Paul employs and attempt to faithfully apply that principle in our setting. The ethic that Paul reiterates throughout 1 Corinthians 6—14 is probably the controlling principle of 1 Corinthians 11, namely that men and women, then and now, should show regard for others' sensibilities in how they act and appear in both the worshiping community and in the world at large. First Corinthians 11, brought across the interpretive bridge, does not mean that women now must cover their heads in our churches when they pray (uncovered hair no longer being sexually suggestive) but that all members of the worshiping community should give thought to how their dress enhances or distracts others from worshiping in a spirit of holiness.

A second qualification is that the comments I make here apply only to Western Christians at this point in history. The claim I am making is not "Paul was wrong—women do not need to cover their hair" but, rather, "Paul was right on the principle of mutual consideration and sexual propriety—and he applied this correctly in his cultural setting." If there are societies in which uncovered hair (or ankles or whatever) in public sends an overtly promiscuous sexual message, then Paul's teaching could apply in a one-to-one correspondence in that setting. Likewise, this teaching is directly applicable to men who dress in a way that sends a sexual message.

A third qualification is that although I write these words in good conscience before God, some may find my approach unseemly. They greet one another with a literal holy kiss as Paul commands four times (Rom 16:16; 1 Cor 16:20; 2 Cor 13:12; 1 Thess 5:26), their women pray with heads covered, and only men wield authority in their churches. For them, anything less than this would be putting human authority above God's authority. Although I respect their consistency and desire to maintain the bonds of Christian fellowship between us, I find their interpretive naiveté unhelpful for Western Christians, particularly those who are seeking ways to interpret the timeless truth of the gospel to our contemporary critical and intellectually sophisticated environment. If we encourage one another to greet the Christian family with a holy kiss, are we not asking our guests to ignore the potentially disastrous consequences that such a nonhygienic practice could have? Surely the cause of Christ is strengthened, not weakened, by greeting one another with holy handshakes and hellos and hugs in light of our current health concerns. So too the cause of Christ is enhanced by acknowledging that Paul wrote for a different cultural setting, words that now must be applied in a different way from how he applied them on his side of the interpretive bridge.

Without going into too much detail, it is possible now to suggest a faithful way to understand and apply 1 Corinthians 14:34-35 and 1 Timothy 2:11-15 on our side of the interpretive crevasse. Paul's teaching about women in both cases has a particular cultural setting and reflects that setting. Paul wanted women in his day to stay silent and exercise no teaching authority for various reasons. Many scholars see Paul's teaching as specific to the situation he was confronting in each letter.[23] For example, Craig Keener points out that these two passages remain in strong tension with the collective fact, demonstrated above, that Paul commends many women as missionary leaders. This dissonance among the letters attributed to Paul should give the impetus we need to identify and contain the culture-specific elements of these passages.[24]

Paul's attitude toward how men and women should behave in public reflects a combination of the specific setting of his readers, the etiquette of the time and his own missionary strategy. He wanted not-yet Christians to receive his God-given message about liberation through Christ without needlessly offending the sensibilities of those in the surrounding community and thus hindering their way to Christ (see 1 Cor 9:19-23). Every missionary struggles with the tension between maintaining biblical integrity and appropriate cultural accommodation for effectiveness, and Paul was no exception.

One objection to this interpretive approach might be that Paul's argument in 1 Timothy 2 against women teaching is grounded on the structure of creation. All that needs to be noted here is that Paul does the same thing with regard to women's head-coverings in 1 Corinthians 11. If we can accept that the requirement that women cover their heads for prayer does not apply now in the same way as it did for Paul, then we can accept in principle that women can and should teach now in our different setting, though Paul argues against its appropriateness in his own setting.

The Use and Abuse of the Bridge

The process of interpretation has been compared to a journey across a bridge. We cross with imagination, attempting to understand Paul's letters as they would have been understood in his day. Then we responsibly and cautiously cross back over that bridge and seek to interpret and apply his message in our own social setting. The bridge must be used—there is no other path—and those who think no bridge is necessary are mistaken. In the chapters that follow, however, some guard rails and guidelines must be spelled out, lest someone think that the bridge can be abused to distort or dilute the authority of the Bible and its power to transform lives. We now turn to the issue of Paul and sexual practices to further explore the problem of Paul and to strengthen and clarify the guard rails on the interpretive bridge.

3

Paul on the *Oprah Winfrey Show:*

The Apostle's Views on Sex & Pleasure

---

*P*aul on the *Oprah Winfrey Show*—just the thought makes me laugh. Can you picture it? There he sits, bald-headed, robed and looking out-of-date as the camera zooms in. The sound of Marvin Gaye's rhythmic "Bring me that feeling, your sexual healing . . ." fades away as Oprah moves through the audience with her microphone and one-liners, probing, embarrassing, going for the sure laugh. It's all about entertainment, and here sits this ancient author and missionary sounding worse than a Victorian prude. He leans forward, adamant that his two-millennia-old Jewish sexual morality with an apocalyptic twist is exactly what the Creator intends for his wayward creatures at the turn of this new millennium.

Does Paul *really* think that singleness without sex is the best path for serious Christians? Yep. Why? The time is short before the Lord's return, and marriage can divide one's energies that should be devoted to the Lord. What if I can't bear the thought? Get married. What if I'm gay? Never heard of "being" gay or lesbian, but the same thing applies to *all* sex outside marriage: Don't do it.

Could Paul survive a session on the *Oprah Winfrey Show,* or would he be booed out of the place? Bishop James Pike candidly said, "Paul was wrong about sex," and Oprah's audience would certainly back this with their boos, oohs, and ahhs. A Gallup Poll would no doubt overwhelmingly support the cleric's view, since by the mideighties one-half of all couples getting married had cohabited. In 1990, 2.9 million households in America were headed by partners who were not married, and a third of those had children under fifteen living with them.[1] The *Oprah Winfrey Show* is a clear indicator of popular opinion, where fast and free sex is the fare of the day, and any suggestion that we bridle our sexual passions and contain them to the marriage bed is thought of as old-fashioned, Victorian, quaint, hung-up.

The topic of a recent *Oprah* show caught the mood of the day. She interviewed gay lovers of married men. The audience response was puzzling. Clearly feminist concerns dominated the discussion, and sexual ethics were overlooked. No one pondered the rightness or wrongness of a sexual liaison with someone else's husband. Rather, the concern most strongly expressed was for the woman who was being taken advantage of (a proper concern): Was she allowed to have the same open access to the extramarital sex *she* desired (a base consideration)?

As these shows go, the tension builds until someone in the audience unleashes the frustrations felt by most. In this case, the group tension was released in a cheer for the audience member who asked the cheating husband, "Do you allow your wife to have a night-a-week of indulgence with other lovers like you grant to yourself?" The concern was not for protecting the sanctity of marriage or for complying with God-given sexual mores; it was an almost petty concern for *quid pro quo*—if *he* gets sex outside marriage, then *she* should too. Oprah casually could say unchallenged, "I personally have no problem with what you do in your bedroom, as long as you don't hurt anyone else doing it."

It is not the scope of this chapter to challenge that statement, though I strongly disagree with it. The cheated spouses are hurt as well as the participants themselves, but that is another matter. The point is that we live in a society where for many the guiding sexual principle is that it doesn't matter what you do in your bedroom as long as you don't hurt anyone else. A man and woman, or two men or two women, can do as they like, as long as they agree to what they do. Even so, our society does draw a moral line. A man or a woman cannot make this choice with a child because there is power-inequity in the decision. The adult has more power, the playing field is not level, and the child doesn't really have a full part in the decision. These are the dominant sexual rules in our society.[2]

Paul lived in a society with as many diverse sexual viewpoints as are displayed in our time. It was into the varied sexual climate of the Greco-Roman world that Paul planted churches and made disciples. Consequently his views on sex are well-documented in his letters. Although his world differed in some key respects from ours, his notions—in places—were as countercultural then as they are now.

We now look at what he said about sex and discover that he is not much of an individualist in this regard. He stands in a long Judeo-Christian tradition with consistent views on the subject of the appropriate context of sexual encounter and the God-given nature of pleasure.

Paul on Sex

Paul roundly condemned sexual contact that violated three concerns: the sanctity of the marriage bed, the commands of God intended to keep us pure, and the will of God in the design of the created heterosexual order. These three he labels adultery, sexual immorality (or fornication) and "against nature," respectively.[3] The real-life installment of the *Oprah Winfrey Show* demonstrated little concern for the first and no awareness of the second or third, but these are the concerns that drive Paul's views about sex. In Paul's earliest letter, we have a clear summary of his thoughts on sex:

> For you know what instructions we gave you through the Lord Jesus. For this is the will of God, your sanctification: that you abstain from fornication *[porneia]*; that each one of you know how to control your own body in holiness and honor, not with lustful passion, like the Gentiles who do

not know God; that no one wrong or exploit a brother or sister in this matter, because the Lord is an avenger in all these things, just as we have already told you beforehand and solemnly warned you. For God did not call us to impurity but in holiness. Therefore whoever rejects this rejects not human authority but God, who also gives his Holy Spirit to you. (1 Thess 4:2-8)

This passage is not hard to unpack. God's will is our "sanctification," that is, the moral purity that results in our lives when Christ indwells us and empowers us to live according to his direction. The immediate implication of sanctification is that we abstain from *porneia,* which should be translated "sexual immorality" or "fornication" and which includes for Paul all sexual encounters outside marriage. In classical Greek (fifth-fourth century B.C.E.), *porneia* referred to prostitution, but by the time of Paul it had come to be used as an umbrella term that summarized all sexual deeds regarded as immoral.[4] Paul uses *porneia* in a general sense for sexually immoral acts (Gal 5:19; Col 3:5; 1 Thess 4:3), and in various contexts he includes incest (1 Cor 5:1), homoerotic behavior (1 Cor 6:9; 1 Tim 1:10) and prostitution (1 Cor 6:13-20). These come under the umbrella term of *porneia,* but they are not the full extent of the sexual practices he rejects.

The most revealing passage about what Paul considers sexually immoral is 1 Corinthians 7:2, where he contrasts *porneia* with the sexual intimacy of a marriage relationship (also see 1 Cor 6:16-18).[5] Thus, for Paul, "sexual immorality" includes all sexual intercourse outside marriage; marriage is the only appropriate place for sex.[6] In 1 Thessalonians 4:2-8, the result of conversion to Christ is the ability given by the Spirit to keep oneself from sexual immorality (vv. 3-4; compare Gal 5:16-25), and it is "the will of God" for our moral purification.

Thessalonica was a somewhat typical Greek town under Roman control, located in the north of Greece in Macedonia. Paul gave his converts there advice that was needed in all the Greco-Roman towns where he planted churches: "Each one of you [should] know how to control your own body in holiness and honor, not with lustful passion, like the Gentiles who do not know God" (vv. 4-5). In this phrase we get a sense of the sexual climate of

Paul's time, which can be confirmed from other literature, art and vase paintings. Many Gentiles were quite free in their display of nudity and very open in their expression of sexual appetites. Paul, however, appeals to their sense of "holiness" and "honor" in adopting new sexual standards as a result of their new life in Christ. The appeal to honor is understandable, as this was a key Greek value. For most Greeks, shame was more distasteful than guilt, and the avoidance of it was an effective motivator. Paul combines this with a concern for "holiness," a biblical notion of conformity with God's commands, which were thought to reflect God's character (see v. 7). Holiness in sexual matters is very serious to Paul because he believes that it is very serious to God: "Whoever rejects this rejects not human authority but God, who also gives the Holy Spirit to you" (v. 8). Reference to the *Holy* Spirit underlines Paul's emphasis on holiness by referring to this aspect of God's character.

Paul believes that he can confidently tell these converts, who were reared in a lax sexual environment, to control themselves because he believes that the indwelling Holy Spirit gives them self-control, a direct "fruit of the Spirit," which results from giving themselves to Christ (Gal 5:22-24). This theme emerges again and again in Paul's letters: "Shun *porneia*. . . . Your body is a temple of the Holy Spirit" (1 Cor 6:18-19); "Do not gratify the desires of the flesh" (Gal 5:16); "Put to death . . . whatever in you is earthly: *porneia*, impurity, passion, evil desire, and greed" (Col 3:5). His viewpoint is clearly the "traditional" view that sex is for marriage, not merely for personal gratification.

A test case can be taken from 1 Corinthians 5—7, where Paul mentions several unacceptable kinds of sexual behavior and concludes by identifying the marriage bed as the proper place for sexual relations. Paul expresses shock at what was happening in the Corinthian church:

> It is actually reported that there is sexual immorality *[porneia]* among you, and of a kind that is not found even among pagans; for a man is living with his father's wife. And you are arrogant! Should you not rather have mourned, so that he who has done this would have been removed from among you? (1 Cor 5:1-2)

Since "sexual immorality" *(porneia)* is a catchall term that Paul uses here to refer to incest, it is clear that Paul sees two problems in the Corinthian church: *porneia,* and a boastful attitude about its presence (1 Cor 5:2, 6). Apparently the Corinthians touted this incestuous relationship (which would shock even Greco-Roman sensibilities) as a sign of their freedom in Christ, a misunderstanding that Paul has to correct more than once in the chapters that follow (compare 1 Cor 6:12; 8:1, 13; 10:23-24). Paul confronts the Corinthians with one of his strongest assertions of authority, insisting twice that they expel this man from the fellowship.

We should read 1 Corinthians 5:3-5 from the Corinthians' point of view when the letter was first read in their hearing. Paul's "presence" with the Corinthians is his spiritual presence conveyed by the power of Christ when the letter is read aloud to them:[7]

> For though absent in body, I am present in spirit; and as if present I have already pronounced judgment in the name of the Lord Jesus on the man who has done such a thing. When you are assembled, and my spirit is present with the power of our Lord Jesus, you are to hand this man over to Satan for the destruction of the flesh, so that his spirit may be saved in the day of the Lord. (1 Cor 5:3-5)

Outside the Christian community is the sphere of darkness and Satan. Expulsion from the community exposes the man to spiritual danger and ultimately to destruction.[8] Paul makes this point clear in the punch line of the chapter: "Drive out the wicked person from among you" (1 Cor 5:13). These drastic measures were required because the spiritual well-being of the whole church was at stake. The Corinthian boasting would permeate the whole community, so he warns, "Your boasting is not a good thing. Do you not know that a little yeast leavens the whole batch of dough? Clean out the old yeast so that you may be a new batch, as you really are unleavened" (vv. 6-7). The harsh treatment itself seems to be remedial, with the hope expressed that ultimately the man, like the prodigal son, will return to his senses before the return of the Lord. (The situation as it later developed might be referred to in 2 Cor 2:5-11; if that is the case, Paul's strategy for reform worked.)

In the next chapter (1 Cor 6), Paul confronts various sins, including a shopping list of sexual practices: those who practice sexual immorality *(pornoi);* those who commit adultery *(moichoi);* both active and passive participants in homosexual behavior (*arsenokoitai, malakoi;* vv. 9-10); and sexual relations with prostitutes (vv. 13-20). "Sexual immorality" is not the only topic of discussion (Paul also addresses intramural lawsuits, idolatry, stealing, lying, drunkenness and improper speech), but the theme of sexual morality in Christ runs through chapters 5—7. It culminates in a discussion of marriage as the proper place for sexual intercourse (1 Cor 7). In Paul's view, sex is for marriage and marriage is for sex. All other options are *porneia.*

Paul on Pleasure

Does this mean that Paul is against people having pleasure, as the Dud and Pete sketch at the beginning of this book suggests? "Stop having fun. . . . Signed, Saint Paul"? This requires some careful handling of several passages, but at the outset it should be underlined that, although Paul did not say much about sex as created for pleasure, it is clear that he agreed with his Jewish heritage in this regard. His lack of emphasis on this theme is easily explained: his Greco-Roman converts do not appear to have needed instruction on pleasure. Generally they knew the self-reinforcing benefits of pleasure and needed to learn limits to their appetites.[9]

Paul's letters are written to instruct them in the implications of their baptism into Christ, and if he comes off as a naysayer this is mostly because that is what this pastoral situation demanded. The fact that Paul does not often discuss the God-given goodness of pleasure within certain limits does not mean that Paul was an "ascetic," a person who practices severe self-discipline and forgoes all pleasure. Rather, he seems typically Jewish in his belief in the essential goodness of creation, so he urges, "Eat whatever is sold in the meat market without raising any question on the ground of conscience, for 'the earth and its fullness are the Lord's' " (1 Cor 10:25-26). Though Paul seems very un-Jewish in this casual attitude toward the meat market (one must read all of 1 Cor 8—10 to feel the full force of his nuanced argument), it reflects a positive Jewish view of the created order. We can suppose that Paul affirms (and certainly never denies) the biblical affirmation of sexual pleasure:

Your lips cover me with kisses; your love is better than wine. There is a fragrance about you. . . . No woman could keep from loving you. Take me with you, and we'll run away; be my king and take me to your room. We will be happy together, drink deep, and lose ourselves in love. (Song 1:2-4 TEV)

In 1 Timothy, for example, he stands against those who "forbid marriage and demand abstinence from foods, which God created to be received with thanksgiving by those who believe and know the truth. For everything created by God is good, and nothing is to be rejected, provided it is received with thanksgiving; for it is sanctified by God's word and by prayer" (1 Tim 4:3-5). Even so, some things Paul says could be misconstrued as statements that oppose pleasure as such.

The confusion is partly related to Paul's use of the word *flesh (sarx)* to refer to a range of notions from physical matter, the human body and the human race to a very negative usage that means "rebellious human nature." For example, the (misunderstood) impression of Galatians 5:16-26 could be thought to denigrate human pleasure: "Live by the Spirit, I say, and do not gratify the desires of the flesh" (v. 16). If by "flesh" Paul meant "the human body," this statement sounds stark; that is, the Spirit-directed person does not fulfill the desires of the human body for physical pleasure. Seeking a sumptuous meal would be ruled out for the Christian. But that is not what Paul meant in this context as he goes on to list what the "works of the flesh" are: "fornication, impurity, licentiousness, idolatry, sorcery, enmities, strife, jealousy, anger, quarrels, dissensions, factions, envy, drunkenness, carousing, and things like these" (5:19-21). It is readily apparent that Paul is not putting down pleasure but is opposing pursuit of things that are done by those who "gratify the desires of the [rebellious human nature within them]." This rebelliousness must be what verse 24 is referring to also: "Those who belong to Christ Jesus have crucified the flesh with its passions and desires."

A passage in 2 Timothy could be wrongly taken as opposing pleasure as such, contrasting loving pleasure *(philēdonoi)* with loving God (2 Tim 3:4). Here too, as in the Galatians passage, the context (vv. 2-3) makes clear that Paul is discussing the excesses of those "given over to pleasure," a better translation of *philēdonoi* than the NRSV's and NIV's "lovers of pleasure."

Paul was not against pleasure, as can be seen in his teaching to those who have insatiable sexual urges: "If anyone thinks that he is not behaving properly toward his fiancée, if his passions are strong, and so it has to be, let him marry as he wishes; it is no sin. Let them marry" (1 Cor 7:36). Paul should not be caricatured from this short statement, because this is not all he has to say about marriage. Certainly avoidance of *porneia* is not a good enough reason by itself to make a marriage vow, but Paul addresses this toward those who are engaged to be married. The point is that Paul acknowledges (a) the strong sex drives of some people (compare with v. 37) and (b) that this natural drive for pleasure is strong and is properly expressed in a marriage relationship.

Paul does not allow one's "spiritual life" to be set against the sexual side of the marital relationship. He urges that the single life should be maintained if possible (vv. 7-8, 38),[10] but he does not want to be understood as against the proper expression of sexuality within marriage. Lest his high view of singleness should be misconstrued, he explicitly says to those who are already married, "Do not deprive one another [of sexual intercourse] except perhaps by agreement for a set time, to devote yourselves to prayer, and then come together again, so that Satan may not tempt you because of your lack of self-control" (v. 5). This is not opposed to his biblical heritage: "Find your joy with the girl you married—pretty and graceful as a deer. Let her charms keep you happy; let her surround you with her love" (Prov 5:18-19 TEV). It is obvious that some Corinthians needed no such encouragement, and Paul's restraint must be read in light of the situation that evoked his letter.

That is true also when Paul reacts to those in Colossae who were teaching an austere approach to pleasure. In opposing this view as well, he attacks the notion in strong terms:

If with Christ you died to the elemental spirits of the universe, why do you live as if you still belonged to the world? Why do you submit to regulations, "Do not handle, Do not taste, Do not touch"? All these regulations refer to things that perish with use; they are simply human commands and teachings. These have indeed an appearance of wisdom in promoting self-imposed piety, humility, and severe treatment of the body, but they are of no value in checking self-indulgence. (Col 2:20-23)

Paul was not an ascetic. For him, severe self-restrictions were no real aid in combating self-indulgence in things that are against God's will (see also Rom 7:7-25). Rather than focusing on willing oneself out of sin, Paul's instruction is to dwell on Christ: "So if you have been raised with Christ, seek the things that are above, where Christ is, seated at the right hand of God. Set your minds on things that are above, not on things that are on earth, for you have died, and your life is hidden with Christ in God" (Col 3:1-3). Paul's counter-cultural stance, then and now, was not against pleasure but against the seeking of pleasure beyond the bounds of Christ-controlled self-restraint.

The problem that Paul's views on sex pose for many people today is that they have sampled and therefore savor the temporary pleasures of sexual liaisons and the sexually explicit movies, magazines and television programs that proliferate today. Some have become too tethered to these pleasures to hear the liberating message that such things are actually bondage (Rom 6) and that obedience to Christ's will in these matters, empowered by the Holy Spirit, brings true liberty, pleasure and fulfillment. In other words, it is not so much that Paul's comments on sexuality are a problem; it is that his views—if followed—cut against the acquired habits and tastes of so many people in our sex-crazed society. Television, billboards, movies and mainstream newspapers and magazines long ago went beyond "presenting the beauty of the human body" to actively exploiting sexual innuendo and explicit and shocking pictures for profit.

Although our culture rightly repudiates date-rape, sex-offenders and the like, it is puzzling to see how silent society and the church remain on the other issues that daily fuel the hormonal fires of a sex-maniacal society. Paul's views, while out of step with the climate of our times, provide a much-needed critique and the grounds for positive steps to wrest the minds of our youth and children—and ourselves—from the grip of the sex-and-image industry. Perhaps we need to present sexual morality as a cost of discipleship more often than we do—as "the crucible on which saints are made today."[11] Fidelity in marriage and celibacy in singleness demand great effort, but they are worth what they cost, not only to us but to God: "You were bought with a price;

therefore glorify God in your body" (1 Cor 6:20).

Paul's Opposition to Homoerotic Behavior

Paul is against any form of sexuality practiced outside marriage, and consistent with this he explicitly opposes homoerotic practices because, he says, they are against God's will for sexuality and his creation (see Rom 1:26-27; 1 Cor 6:9; 1 Tim 1:10). Paul announces that all humanity is under condemnation because of its sinfulness and that none of us, homoerotic or not, can judge another as worse than ourselves (Rom 2:1-3). The gossiper stands as condemned as the murderer or the arrogant in light of God's high standard of righteousness (vv. 29-32). In fact, Paul's argument in Romans 1 is designed as a rhetorical trap that would especially snare someone schooled in Hellenistic Judaism. The point he makes from it all is that "there is no one who is righteous" by God's standard (Rom 3:10), that "all have sinned and fall short of the glory of God" (v. 23) and that every person desperately needs Jesus Christ as his or her Redeemer (vv. 22, 24). One could say that Paul has an egalitarian view of sin: we are all hopelessly in need of Christ to find God's righteousness.

It is now popular—but unjustified—to assert that Paul, in fact, does not oppose homoeroticism as a part of this general sinfulness of humanity. Two major arguments to this effect have gained a popular enthusiasm that is not supported by the textual evidence. It is worth pausing to dispel the impression that this is an open question. It is not. It is clear that Paul condemns homoerotic practice as severely as he does incest, prostitution, adultery and all forms of "sexual immorality."

The most influential arguments were posed by the gay scholar John Boswell in his *Christianity, Social Tolerance and Homosexuality: Gay People in Western Europe from the Beginning of the Christian Era to the Fourteenth Century.*[12] Though he has had popular influence, few Pauline scholars have agreed with him. Instead, the scholarly consensus on Romans 1 is that Paul clearly condemns homoerotic sexual practice, both male and female:

> Their women exchanged natural intercourse for unnatural, and in the same
> way also the men, giving up natural intercourse with women, were con-

sumed with passion for one another. Men committed shameless acts with men and received in their own persons the due penalty for their error. And since they did not see fit to acknowledge God, God gave them up to a debased mind and to things that should not be done. (vv. 26-28)

How does Boswell get around this? He asserts that this passage is not against innate gays or lesbians ("inverts") having active intercourse with one another; rather, it is against *heterosexuals* crossing over and practicing sex that is unnatural *for them only,* making them "perverts." Boswell thinks that it is not referring to homosexuals who are true to themselves, that is, who practice sex within the bounds of their identity as gays or lesbians. Many writers have been eager to accept this interpretation in order to eliminate from consideration the clearest condemnation of homosexual practice in the Bible.

I can say in the strongest possible terms that Boswell's interpretation of this passage cannot be correct. It is impossible to fit his interpretation with Paul's attitude toward *porneia,* and there is no way an ancient reader could have appreciated an interpretation that turns on the modern notion of inverted homosexuality. There is simply no evidence in antiquity that anyone had a notion of *"being* gay" or *"being* homosexual" by birth or design. The label "homosexual" was not even coined until the second half of the nineteenth century by Hungarian physician Karoly M. Benkert,[13] and the Greek language had no nouns corresponding to the English nouns for "heterosexual" and "homosexual." In an authoritative and thorough study of Greek homosexuality, Oxford classicist Kenneth J. Dover attributes this to the fact that the Greeks assumed that "virtually everyone responds at different times both to homosexual and heterosexual stimuli."[14]

Boswell's interpretation of Romans 1, then, is clearly anachronistic, viewing Romans 1 from a distinctly modern—and Western—view of sexuality and identity. Boswell fails to understand Paul's text from *Paul's* side of the interpretive bridge. Paul, as an ancient, simply could not have understood Boswell's interpretation.[15]

A second influential argument against the traditional understanding of Romans 1 is posed by Robin Scroggs in his book *The New Testament and Homosexuality: Contextual Background for Contemporary Debate.* Scroggs turns the tables and charges that the traditional reading of Romans 1 is anachronistic. His book is devoted to proving that Paul did not and could not have been thinking of anything other than the practice of pederasty, intercourse between an active and older man and a passive boy. Scroggs's own suspicion is that Paul was against the more degrading forms of this practice that employed a young male prostitute *(malakos)* or the sexual domination of a master with his slave.[16]

In this argument, Scroggs takes very seriously *Paul's* side of the interpretive bridge. Pederasty, prostitution and a master's sexual abuse of his slaves are clearly documented as the most common homosexual practices cited in the known literature and portrayed on vase paintings. There are two reasons, however, why we should not accept Scroggs's reconstruction.

First, Paul stands in the long ethical tradition of Judaism that condemned all homosexual practice.[17] This is evident in Paul's coining of the term "those who lie with men" *(arsenokoitai;* "sodomites" NRSV) in 1 Corinthians 6:9 and 1 Timothy 1:10. It is the first use of this term in the Greek language.[18] Scroggs gets credit for showing that Paul derives the parts of this word from the prohibitions against homosexual practice in Leviticus 18:23 (LXX 18:22) and 20:13. Paul's novel contribution to the Greek language combines the two terms found in the Greek version of the Old Testament: *arsēn* = "male," and *koitē* = "bed."[19] Paul thus identifies with this Old Testament tradition in condemning homoeroticism among those practices that exclude one from the kingdom of God, and he asserts that baptism into Christ eliminates homoerotic behavior along with several other forms of sexual immorality and sinful acts (1 Cor 6:9-10; 1 Tim 1:9-10).

This leads to a second and decisive reason why we cannot accept Scroggs's understanding that Romans 1 refers to pederasty: Pederasty occurred between men and boys, but Paul condemns a practice that cannot be identified as pederasty. "Their *women* exchanged natural intercourse for unnatural, and in the same way also the men, giving up natural intercourse with *women*, were consumed with passion for one another" (v. 26). Under no conditions can this verse be reduced to a reference to mere pederasty.

Furthermore, Scroggs cites evidence from other Greek writers, including

Plato, Plutarch and Pseudo-Phocylides, *who refer to female homoerotic acts*.[20] Against Scroggs's contention, there *is* evidence for homoerotic activity that was *not* pederasty. He attempts to dismiss Romans 1:26 with the disclaimer, "What the female part of the slogan may have included is beyond recovery."[21] Hardly. Scroggs has clearly succumbed to the reductionism that he claims he avoids.[22] It is clear from the evidence—which Scroggs himself cites—that Paul could and did have something besides pederasty in mind, and he condemns both male and female homoeroticism as against the will of God.

Homosexuality and the Interpretive Bridge

In the last chapter it was argued that not all of Paul's teaching on women should be applied in the way it was in his day because of the cultural divide that separates us from the hearers to whom these instructions were originally addressed. Some interpreters have taken the same approach to Paul's teaching on homosexual practice, asserting that Paul may have been explicitly against the homoerotic sexual practices of his time and culture, but that does not mean that we should apply his views today. We live on the other end of the interpretive bridge. Paul knew nothing of contemporary gay and lesbian Christian notions of same-sex unions made in the mutuality of love. Therefore, he has nothing to say on the subject, the argument goes.[23]

The principle of cultural translation about the teaching on women has been applied by analogy to homosexual ethics. Some have suggested that just as Paul's prohibitions against women's teaching are disregarded, so too should Paul's teaching on homosexuality. I dismiss this analogy for several reasons and maintain that Paul's views on women need to be translated, whereas his views on homosexual practice remain normative for us.

1. Paul's teaching on women and homosexuality are not of the same order. Paul's views on women's practices in worship have to do with church etiquette, whereas his views on homoerotic behavior have to do with God's created purpose for sex and the normative character of heterosexual marriage. Homoeroticism, like other forms of *porneia* and adultery, assaults God's design for marriage. Translating Paul's church etiquette about women is hardly the same as ignoring the broader biblical view of the sanctity of marriage and the

inappropriateness of sexual intercourse outside marriage.

The contrast of *porneia* with morally acceptable sexual intercourse within marriage (1 Cor 7) sets the issue of homosexual practice within the broader moral fabric of Paul's teaching and that of the Bible. Furthermore, it has been shown that the issue of women's head covering in 1 Corinthians 11 may itself have related to concern about *porneia,* giving the impression that Christians approved of sexual freedom apart from marriage. Although homoerotic practice has been singled out in this chapter, in fact Paul groups it with incest, prostitution, pederasty, stealing, idolatry, gossip and the overarching moral code that he adopts and adapts from Hellenistic Judaism.

2. This leads to a second inadequacy of treating sexual ethics and church etiquette about women in the same way. This is the critical point: The Old and New Testaments and the tradition of the church have been united in a singular position that homoerotic behavior is *porneia* and is against God's will. The Bible teaches one thing about sexuality, a view that historically the church has universally upheld (until recently): Christians are to be faithful in marriage, celibate in singleness. Paul's views on women's head covering in the Corinthian church (1 Cor 11), on the other hand, relate to no broader biblical tradition in a way that is remotely analogous to how his views on homoerotic practice tie in with biblical teaching. Paul himself presents a complicated picture of the role of women leaders in his churches. Paul himself gives examples of women doing things that seem counter to his apparently situation-specific advice about head-coverings and women exercising teaching authority. In other words, Paul gives us reason to pause at universally applying his teaching about women's behavior in 1 Corinthians 11 or 1 Timothy 2. No such ambivalence about homosexual practices exists. There is not a single positive remark about homosexual practice in Paul and the Bible (and the early church for that matter), but there are many examples of women leading the Christian churches.

3. The analogy of homosexual practice and church etiquette for women breaks down for a third reason: As far as the Bible is concerned, *being* a woman is never considered sinful, nor was there condemnation about *being* homosexual, which is an intellectual construct of the last century. The Bible

attacks homoerotic *practice, not being*. The Greek and Hebrew languages do not even have a word that can be translated "homosexual," a point on which English translations have foundered.

Although some lesbian and gay Christians may want to transfer back to Paul the relatively recent notion of "homosexual identity," it is purely anachronistic to treat this as a category Paul would recognize. It is wrong to put into his mouth, "There is neither Jew nor Gentile, male nor female, slave nor free, homosexual nor heterosexual." This illegitimately attempts to take Paul's social comment and transform it into support for the acceptability of homosexual practice. There was never anything *wrong* with being Jew or Gentile, male or female, slave or free, but the latter two are purely modern constructs. One never chose to be any of the first six categories (with the occasional exception of slaves), and it may be that sexual preferences are not chosen either.

One clear distinction needs to be made: Although Paul never condemns *being* a homosexual or having that orientation, he clearly and consistently condemns both heterosexual sex apart from the marriage bed and homosexual practices, which by *biblical* definition must be extramarital.[24] The relevant Pauline analogy is not between heterosexual and homosexual (contemporary categories of sexual identity) but between adulterer, gossip, murderer and one who engages in heterosexual or homoerotic extramarital intimacies (ethical categories of behavior). All these are examples of the behavior that baptism into Christ is meant to transform (1 Cor 6:9-10). Paul gives clear instruction to all those who are not married, whether they see themselves as heterosexual, homosexual, bisexual or something else: they are to remain celibate (1 Cor 7).

4. The clear difference between the culturally limited nature of Paul's comments about women's head-coverings in worship in 1 Corinthians 11 and the crossculturally valid prohibition of homosexual intercourse is underlined by a further observation. The issue of head-coverings appears only in 1 Corinthians 11, so there is no evidence that a crosscultural ethical issue is involved as such. Apparently, Paul's pastoral advice is meant for, and limited to, a situation being faced by the house churches on the Corinthian Isthmus of Greece.

In strong contrast, the prohibitions against homoeroticism are announced in pre-Roman Palestinian Judaism (Leviticus), the Greek-speaking city of Corinth, the culturally distinct Asia Minor (1 Tim 1) and the distant Latin-speaking imperial capital of Rome (Rom 1). Hellenistic Judaism throughout these areas, like Paul, interpreted the Old Testament sexual mores as condemning homoeroticism. These multiple, crosscultural witnesses cause homosexual intercourse to stand in sharp contrast to the issue of women's headcoverings.

5. The contention of Robin Scroggs—that Paul condemned the kind of homosexual practices he knew (pederasty, prostitution and a master's domination of his slave) but that his prohibitions do not apply to the homosexuality that we know on our side of the interpretive bridge—cannot be sustained. The decisive piece of evidence (which Scroggs wrongly dismisses) is that Paul condemns both male *and female* homosexual practices (Rom 1:26-27). Scroggs is well aware that there is little evidence of lesbianism in antiquity, but this has to do with the low status of women and the disinterest of mostly male authors in women's sexuality.[25] This makes Paul's reference to same-sex intercourse between women in Romans 1 even more striking because of its rarity among references to lesbianism in antiquity.

Scroggs simply does not account for this evidence when he wrongly generalizes, "Paul thinks of pederasty, and perhaps the more degraded forms of it, when he is attacking homosexuality."[26] This conclusion cannot account for Paul's mention of women's practice, the intertextuality of Romans 1 and the Genesis creation story, or Paul's coinage of the term "those who lie with men" that draws on the Levitical rather than the Greco-Roman symbolic world. Paul condemns not simply pederasty but homosexual practice in general, and as such his prohibition does carry across the interpretive bridge.[27]

Furthermore, it is questionable that modern homoerotic practices are as far different from those Paul condemns as Scroggs suggests. Scroggs assumes that there is a "model aspired to by the gay community today" (p. 109) that involves a mutuality and caring unlike the dominating practices of pederasty in Paul's day. It is doubtful that the diverse viewpoints among gays and lesbians could be identified as a single model among a unified community. The famous

Bell and Weinberg study suggests the contrary: one-third of gays experience more than a thousand sexual partners in their lifetimes; fewer than 10 percent of gays are in "committed, long-term" relationships.[28] Contemporary gay relationships, statistically speaking, do not approximate an analogy to the biblical ideal of the permanency of one man and one woman. In fact, McWhirter and Mattison found in their study of one hundred stable male couples that none of them (0 percent) were sexually monogamous after being together for five years. They conclude—contrary to Scripture—that monogamy is an unnatural state and that to be gay is to be "nonmonogamous."[29] Paul's teaching is indisputably against such a viewpoint.

6. A sixth analogy between homoerotic practice and church etiquette for women is the not-very-often argument: "The Bible does not treat this issue very often and so it should not be weighted too heavily in our ethics." (The same sort of approach is sometimes taken in the discussion of the Bible and women.) This analogy cannot be taken seriously. Paul's views on homosexual practice were presented in a cultural environment in which negative judgments on the practice were becoming commonplace, appearing in Greco-Roman popular moral-philosophical literature as well.[30] Paul did not need to refer often to something that he could take for granted, and his argument *from* the wrongness of homosexual practice in Romans 1 suggests that his viewpoint was rhetorical middle ground, acceptable to his readers and employed to lead them *from* (rather than *to*) the unnaturalness of homosexuality—which they accepted—to another conclusion: All creation is corrupted by sin, and all creation stands in need of a Redeemer. A comparison can be made with robbery. Just because Paul mentions robbery only three times (Rom 2:22; 1 Cor 5:10-11; 6:10), no one would conclude that it wasn't really a very serious issue for him. The number of times an issue is mentioned may have nothing to do with its seriousness or the weight it should be given.

Thus it should not be thought that the last chapter's treatment of the interpretive bridge and women should be seen as a Pandora's box that neutralizes the authority of Scripture in other matters. What was argued there is that Paul's etiquette for women in his culture needs to be adapted to proper etiquette in our culture. *Porneia* is not in this category. Then and now the standard is simply stated: Fidelity in marriage, celibacy in singleness.

The Interpretive Bridge and AIDS

A cautionary note needs to be sounded. Stigmatization of homosexuality as a worse sort of sin than others is not supported by Scripture. Paul refers to homoerotic sex in Romans 1, not because it is a special form of sinfulness but because it was rhetorically effective with his readers in drawing the conclusion of Romans 2:1ff: "Therefore you have no excuse, whoever you are . . ." Homosexual practice is not of a worse order of sinfulness but provides the rhetorical trap that draws the readers into an agreement with the sinfulness of all humanity. This observation is supported by the two other references to homoerotic behavior in Paul's letters (1 Cor 6:9-10; 1 Tim 1:10). In both cases it appears as one sin on a shopping list of sins (so-called vice lists) utilized by Paul to illustrate the human sinfulness from which Christ redeems us.

That homosexuality does not deserve to be singled out as qualitatively worse than other sins is underlined by its absence in Paul's several other catalogs of vices (for example, Rom 1:29-31; Gal 5:19-21; 1 Cor 5:10-11).[31] In other words, Paul's text—understood from Paul's side of the bridge—cannot be used to justify the singling out of homosexuality on our side of the bridge. Boswell's *Christianity, Social Tolerance and Homosexuality* correctly demonstrates—even if we disagree sharply with his interpretation of Romans 1—that the historical Christian persecution of homosexuals is not supported by the teaching of the Scriptures.

A particularly cruel misuse of Paul is the contemporary diatribe against homosexuality that interprets acquired immune deficiency syndrome (AIDS) as God's singling out of homosexuals as particularly heinous sinners whom he is now punishing physically. This approach interprets Romans 1:27 from this heartless perspective and supposes that AIDS is God's specific punishment upon homosexuals: "Men committed shameless acts with men and received in their own persons the due penalty for their error."

There are two problems with this rendering. First, AIDS is a very recent phenomenon, and Paul refers to something that was already happening in his time. Second, Romans 1:28 interprets what this "due penalty" is. It does not refer to physical disease but to same-sex desire, as well as the other examples listed in verses 29-32, which come as a consequence of rejecting God: "And since they did not see fit to acknowledge God, God gave them up to a debased mind and to things that should not be done." Paul is not referring to AIDS as a consequence of homosexual practice but homosexual practice and all sinful practice as a consequence of the rejection of God. In other words, Paul asserts in verse 27 that "sexual perversion is its own inevitable penalty."[32] The context of verse 27 makes that explicit, and this interpretation has been acknowledged as correct throughout the history of the church.[33] Paul was not referring to sexually transmitted disease, and it is misguided to enlist Romans 1:27 as support for this cruelty.

There is a sense in which the New Testament teaches that physical ailments can be a consequence of one's own or one's parents' sinfulness (for example, Mk 2:1-12; Jn 9:1-3), but there is no mention of that in Romans 1:27. Much heart disease is directly related to gluttony, and many injuries and diseases are related to specific acts. Indeed, sexually transmitted diseases are largely avoidable. But AIDS is transmitted by more than sexual means, and if we are going to attach particular diseases to particular sins, we should go all the way and identify the behavioral source of diabetes, stroke, cancer and the like. Few show a willingness to do this, suggesting that the misuse of Romans 1:27 against AIDS is perhaps more reflective of common bigotry against gays and lesbians rather than an evenhanded application of biblical theology. Nevertheless, we should not blame Paul for the misuse to which Romans 1:27 has been put, since he did not mean the comment as an explanation for the origin of AIDS.

The Episode Ends

So how would Paul fare on *Oprah*? He would have to defend himself against misinterpretations of his teaching (such as AIDS), but in other cases he would be adamant that traditional views about sex and marriage are the only way to honor the God of the Bible. His closing appeal would surely reflect his missionary zeal that all people be reconciled to God through Christ. He might say something like his words to the Roman Christians:

> I appeal to you therefore, brothers and sisters, by the mercies of God, to present your bodies as a living sacrifice, holy and acceptable to God, which is your spiritual worship. Do not be conformed to this world, but be transformed by the renewing of your minds, so that you may discern what is the will of God—what is good and acceptable and perfect. (Rom 12:1-2)

In a society that is becoming more and more characterized by sexual addictions, sex crimes and the degrading of persons by portraying their bodies in video meat markets, this advice is timely and even redemptive. To the Christians in the audience he might ask rhetorically, as he put it to his Corinthian converts, "Do you not know that your body is a temple of the Holy Spirit within you, which you have from God, and that you are not your own?" (1 Cor 6:19). The practice of self-restraint in sexual matters for Paul is directly related to what Christ has done for us: "For you were bought with a price; therefore glorify God in your body" (v. 20).

It is likely, too, that the apostle who majored on God's grace and mercy would show an awareness that some in the audience would not have measured up to the standards he espoused. In a context where he uses homosexual practice along with *porneia* and lying (among other things) to illustrate human sinfulness (1 Tim 1:9-11), Paul turns the tables on himself and includes his own despicable sinfulness within the reach of Christ's redemptive grasp:

> I am grateful to Christ Jesus our Lord, who has strengthened me, because he judged me faithful and appointed me to his service, even though I was formerly a blasphemer, a persecutor, and a man of violence. But I received mercy because I had acted ignorantly in unbelief, and the grace of our Lord overflowed for me with the faith and love that are in Christ Jesus. The saying is sure and worthy of full acceptance, that Christ Jesus came into the world to save sinners—of whom I am the foremost. But for that very reason I received mercy, so that in me, as the foremost, Jesus Christ might display the utmost patience, making me an example to those who would come to believe in him for eternal life. (1 Tim 1:12-16)

Paul wants the group he mentioned in the verses that introduce this passage to know that Christ's gracious patience and forgiveness extends to them, "for the godless and sinful, for the unholy and profane, for those who kill their father or mother, for murderers, [the sexually immoral, those who practice homosexuality,] slave traders, liars, perjurers" (1 Tim 1:9-11). As Christ saved Paul, "the chief of sinners," and turned him from hating Christ and killing Christians, so Christ can redeem and reform even those who watch *Oprah*.

4

Single Paul & His Married Followers

I talk to a lot of couples about getting married. When we plan the wedding ceremony I always ask, "Is there anything you have seen at another wedding that you especially want to see happen at yours, or something you want to avoid at all costs?" Many brides (but not once a groom) respond, "I don't want anything in the vows about obeying my husband." I am always relieved if that is their only concern, because, frankly, I have never witnessed a ceremony where a bride pledged to obey her husband. Apparently many brides have witnessed the slavery-pledge (in an old movie?) or have had nightmares about it or just do not want to chance it.

Of course, Paul is often blamed for this mysterious obedience clause that disappeared from wedding services some time ago. Nowhere does he say that wives should obey their husbands, but he still gets the blame. He urges "submission," but never does he tell a wife that she should *obey* her husband, a notion he reserves for children's relationship to their parents and slaves' relationship to their masters (Eph 6:1-8; Col 3:20-22).

Even when we remove the mistaken notions about Paul's teaching on marriage, what he does say is hard for many to take. It is even harder to swallow when mention is made that Paul was not married (1 Cor 7:7-8). What right does he have to set the rules for modern marriages when he did not participate in an ancient one? Though this last accusation carries some force, the Bible is silent on the issue of Paul's past: we are not told if Paul was always single or if he was previously married and later widowed or divorced. These are questions the text never answers. Some have supposed that since Paul was a Pharisee he probably married at age eighteen, due to the remark of the rabbi Jehuda ben Tema: "To scripture at five, to the Mishnah at ten, to the commandments at thirteen, to the Talmud at fifteen and to the bridal chamber at eighteen" (Abot 5:21). This source comes from sometime after Paul's childhood, and there is no way of knowing to what degree Paul lived out this five-stage plan.[1]

A fair understanding of Paul's views about marriage is best discovered by a thoughtful trip across the interpretive bridge to his cultural setting and by a careful and close reading of what he actually says. The passages in question are found in Colossians and Ephesians and are followed in both cases by instructions to parents and children, masters and slaves.

And whatever you do, in word or deed, do everything in the name of the Lord Jesus, giving thanks to God the Father through him. Wives, be subject to your husbands, as is fitting in the Lord. Husbands, love your wives and never treat them harshly. (Col 3:17-18)

Be subject to one another out of reverence for Christ. Wives, be subject to your husbands as you are to the Lord. For the husband is the head of the wife just as Christ is the head of the church, the body of which he is the Savior. Just as the church is subject to Christ, so also wives ought to be, in everything, to their husbands. Husbands, love your wives, just as Christ loved the church and gave himself up for her, in order to make her holy by cleansing her with the washing of water by the word, so as to present the church to himself in splendor, without a spot or wrinkle or anything of the kind—yes, so that she may be holy and without blemish.

In the same way, husbands should love their wives as they do their own bodies. He who loves his wife loves himself. For no one ever hates his own body, but he nourishes and tenderly cares for it, just as Christ does for the church, because we are members of his body. "For this reason a man will leave his father and mother and be joined to his wife, and the two will become one flesh." This is a great mystery, and I am applying it to Christ and the church. Each of you, however, should love his wife as himself, and a wife should respect her husband. (Eph 5:21-33)

These texts may be the most rationalized, rejected and ignored passages in Paul's letters. To illustrate, while writing this chapter I wanted some feedback from women on these portions of Scripture, so I asked two married women if they would mind responding to something Paul said. After they agreed, I started reciting the passages. Both women began laughing. In fact, it was difficult for me to get them to remain serious on the subject. These women are both committed Christians, devoted to prayer, avid in Bible reading, leaders in their churches, concerned for the poor and the lost. Yet these passages are difficult for them to take seriously.

On another occasion, at a broadly evangelical church, I chose to speak on Ephesians 5 and was quietly congratulated afterwards for my courage—not for the position I took but that *I spoke on this passage at all!* Another invitation allowed me to address these texts at a women's Bible study, where the response was one of general agreement with the views I develop later in this chapter. Even so, I was cautioned not to let their pastor know they agreed with me!

If Paul's views on sex would draw boos and hisses on the *Oprah Winfrey Show,* his views on the marriage relationship have as low an approval rating within the church. Nevertheless, many thoughtful people have grappled with these passages in an attempt to interpret their relevance for our day. I turn now to a discussion of some common approaches to these passages that scholars call "household codes."

Recent Approaches to Household Codes in Colossians and Ephesians

There are many people for whom these passages reflect the correct order of things and create no problem. For others of us, however, these passages are among the most troublesome, if not for our own conscience, then in our interactions with not-yet Christians whom we want to interest in the gospel. Three current approaches to these passages are worth reviewing and weighing in our attempt to grapple with Paul from our crosscultural perspective.

1. "Paul didn't say it, I don't believe it, that settles it." In the early 1800s German scholar Ferdinand Christian Baur proposed that Paul wrote only four of the thirteen letters that bear his name: Romans, 1 and 2 Corinthians, and Galatians (the so-called *Hauptbriefe,* or principal letters). This legacy has continued to affect Pauline scholarship ever since as scholars have pondered and debated, attacked and defended the authorship and authenticity of each letter. If a vote of academic scholars were taken today, Philippians, 1 Thessalonians and Philemon would fill out the list of the seven undisputed Pauline letters. The authentically Pauline character of the remaining six (Colossians, 2 Thessalonians, Ephesians, 1 Timothy, 2 Timothy and Titus) is debated by scholars. Colossians and 2 Thessalonians are less disputed than Ephesians, but 1 and 2 Timothy and Titus, usually lumped together as "the Pastoral Epistles," are widely believed to have been written after Paul's lifetime and put in his name (see notes 1 and 3 from chapter two).

If these scholars are right, Paul himself is let off the hook for the views of marriage expressed in Ephesians, Colossians and the Pastorals, and the balance of blame is shifted to anonymous authors who have published their ideas in the name of Paul. A recent example of this approach is Robert Jewett, who considers only the seven undisputed letters for his portrait of the "true historical Paul." In *Paul, the Apostle to America,* he chastises others who do not accept his reconstruction: "Conservative authors are unwilling to distinguish between authentic and inauthentic Pauline writings, and thus are unable to separate the true historical Paul from the despised, authoritarian framework provided by Acts and the Pastoral Epistles."[2] This sort of statement, though usually expressed in less patronizing and caustic terms, is accepted by many Pauline scholars. But not all scholars who assert that Paul wrote all thirteen letters are "conservative,"[3] and the polarity between these writings suggested by Jewett is not accurate.

First Corinthians 5, for example, points to a highly authoritarian "true historical Paul," and we are still left with the apparently "sexist" nature of 1 Corinthians 14:33-36. The sources do not divide as cleanly as Jewett's caricature suggests. Even if Jewett were right about the authorship question, he does not consistently carry forward his program. In one instance, he accepts that Colossians was designed by Paul, but a short while later he sharply separates the content of Colossians from consideration of what Paul believed.[4] This seems arbitrary and unhelpful. It is unhelpful in coming to grips with Paul's teaching about marriage in Colossians and Ephesians for at least two reasons.

First of all, fewer scholars question the authenticity of Colossians, and Jewett himself is ambivalent. Of those who do have doubts, many think that it was written by one of Paul's disciples during his imprisonment (explaining the variations of style and vocabulary), even under Paul's auspices (explaining the typically Pauline themes and vocabulary and the autograph in 4:18).[5] Ephesians is more of a mixed bag, but there is nothing approaching unanimity among scholars that Ephesians is inauthentic.[6] The many points of contact between distinctive Pauline vocabulary and thought in these two letters and Paul's other letters is usually explained by attributing them to Paul's disciples or to "the Pauline school."

If, for sake of argument, we grant that Colossians and Ephesians were written by Paul's disciples, then we must give full weight to this observation. These disciples constitute highly authoritative, very early interpreters of what Paul thought about these subjects, and presumably they were successful in putting their words into Paul's mouth, so to speak, because their words have been recognized as Pauline.[7] As the earliest interpreters of Paul—and I am not convinced that they were not written by Paul himself—their teaching on marriage and slavery cannot be easily dismissed as unrepresentative of Paul's teaching.[8] Thus, for the purposes of this study, the name *Paul* is used to refer to the persona depicted and described in the thirteen letters and Acts. After all, one person's "Deutero-Paul" is another's "true Paul"!

A second reason this scholastic approach is unhelpful is that it disregards the problem that these passages continue to present to the church, since these letters remain part of the Christian canon of Scripture (whatever scholars may think about their authorship). Although it may satisfy some to simply dismiss the so-called deutero-Pauline letters, the church is still left with the task of coming to grips with its canon. If some critical scholars make the problem of Paul into the problem-of-a-man-called-Paul-who-wrote-Colossians-Ephesians-and-the-Pastoral-Epistles, the church, which takes seriously its canon, must grapple with this man-called-Paul, regardless of the nuances of academic discussions about the relationships of the thirteen letters. Ephesians, Colossians, 2 Thessalonians, 1 and 2 Timothy and Titus have been enshrined in our canon as Scripture and must be dealt with as such.

2. *The apologetic purpose of the household codes.* Another approach to these passages is to minimize their offense by arguing for their purpose not so much as ethical statements but as propaganda to make Christianity more palatable to its Greco-Roman observers. "Christianity had a reputation as a domestic trouble maker," says Abraham Malherbe.[9] This was particularly the case in divided households, where a slave or a spouse became a Christian and their loyalties became divided. Furthermore, early Christian apologetics (reasoned defenses of the Christian faith to non-Christians) followed in the tradition of Judaism's need to defend its life in society against charges that it was antisocial. The early Christian church was effective in its mission to women and slaves, and this had political implications in a society where both groups were expected to accept the religion of the male head of the household, the *paterfamilias.*

Since the family was considered the building block of the city, the undermining of the male's authority could be taken as tantamount to civil treason. "Upset the order of the home, people believed, and the whole society was in trouble."[10] David Balch has made the compelling case that the domestic teaching in 1 Peter 2:11—3:22 serves just such an apologetic social function, to defend Christians as socially acceptable and no threat to the social order (see 1 Pet 2:12; 3:15-16). By being subordinate, Christian wives and slaves would silence criticism of the early Christians whom 1 Peter addresses.[11]

Does this later use of the household code in 1 Peter inform us about how Paul employs these pieces in Colossians and Ephesians?[12] In the earlier Colossians there is a side glance at social impressions (Col 4:5), but overall the teaching here focuses on behavior that is fitting for those who are "in Christ." So, for example, the instructions to slaves are not just for appearances but are placed in the context of what God desires of them when no one is watching (Col 3:22-24; so also Eph 6:6-8). If a social context is sought as to why Colossians stresses household order, it is probably best found in relation to Paul's opponents, who emphasized asceticism and visionary experiences and who needed to be brought down to earth and reminded of their ethical responsibilities in day-to-day living.[13] Neither in Ephesians nor in Colossians is there the evidence of 1 Peter that the recipients were facing societal criticisms and that this was a prime factor in the domestic code's usage. Instead, both Pauline letters assert what were thought to be ideal social relations based on Christian theological principles, even if those ideal social relations largely mirror the accepted social arrangements of Greco-Roman households.[14]

3. Paul modifies commonly held chauvinistic values. A third approach to these passages is that Paul's views reflect his interaction with and adaptation of the values of his surrounding culture. There was a consistent patriarchal pattern throughout Greco-Roman society that assumed the subordination of wives to husbands, children to parents and slaves to masters. This pattern is undergirded by Aristotle's political philosophy, which left an indelible imprint on Greco-Roman society. Aristotle asserted—and Greco-Roman culture embodied—that marriage, parenthood and slavery are foundational to society:

> The investigation of everything should begin with its smallest parts, and the smallest and primary parts of the household are master and slave, husband and wife, father and children. We ought therefore to examine the proper constitution and character of each of the three relationships, I mean that of mastership, that of marriage and thirdly the progenitive relationship.[15]

It is no surprise that Paul treats marriage, parenting and slavery together, given that these topics were often treated together in his cultural context. This same pattern was embodied in the Hellenistic Judaism of Paul's day.

Philo, an older contemporary of Paul's who wrote from Alexandria (the largest settlement of Jews outside Palestine), defended the social respectability of the Jews, insisting that they respect mother and father and that wives serve their husbands: "Any of them whom you attack with inquiries about their ancestral institutions can answer you rapidly and easily. The husband seems competent to transmit knowledge of the laws to his wife, the father to his children, the master to his slaves."[16]

Josephus, a Palestinian-born politician, military commander and historian, was a younger contemporary of Paul's with very similar views. Writing near the end of the first century as a Roman slave, he defends Judaism in the tract *Against Apion*. Like Philo, he defends the acceptability of Jewish marital practices to Roman sensibilities: "The woman, says the Law, is in all things inferior to the man. Let her accordingly be submissive, not for her humiliation, but that she may be directed, for the authority has been given by God to the man."[17]

In light of the social context, Colossians 3:17-18 and Ephesians 5:21-33, except for their Christian grounding and motivation, are typical, socially conservative views on household management that could be found throughout the empire of Paul's day. Though there is no one model of marriage from the Greco-Roman world, a passage by Areius Didymus from the first century B.C.E. gives the flavor of Paul's social context:

> The man has the rule of this house by nature. For the deliberative faculty in a woman is inferior, in children it does not yet exist, and it is completely foreign to slaves. Rational household management, which is the controlling of a house and of those things related to the house, is fitting for a man. Belonging to this are fatherhood, the art of marriage, being a master, and moneymaking.[18]

Paul nowhere puts down the intelligence of women, children or slaves, but he does seem to presume a household hierarchy with the husband/father/master at the head of the pyramid. Since Paul's views in Colossians and Ephesians are culturally consistent with those found in his Greco-Roman social world, that should lead us to examine closely how he appropriates, shapes and even critiques this culturally acceptable teaching, and it reminds us that we live on the other side of the cultural divide, where Paul's views to the ancients must be interpreted and adapted to our new cultural context.

Close Reading and Careful Crossing

The first thing a close reading of these passages in Paul reveals, in light of the subordinationist culture in which he was situated, is that Ephesians 5:21 frames the household teaching in a remarkable, countercultural way: "Be subject to one another out of reverence for Christ." With this verse Paul potentially upends the authoritarian pyramid of his day, making mutual submission a mark of devotion to Christ and potentially downgrading hierarchical subjugation.

Ephesians 5:21 announces a social restructuring, but it remains in tension with what follows. In Ephesians 5:22—6:8, the traditional views on the hierarchical relations of husband-wife, parent-child and master-slave appear to be reaffirmed and the old social structures upheld. Scholars have attempted to harmonize 5:21 with 5:22—6:8 in two main ways, both of which acknowledge that 5:21 is in tension with what follows.[19]

One approach to the tension is to view Ephesians 5:21 as a general heading for what follows. In this approach, the verse is not about *mutual* submission ("Be subject to one another") but about *appropriate* submission, that is, submitting yourselves to those you should—wives to husbands, children to parents, slaves to masters. This interpretation of 5:21 in light of what follows gives too little credence to the force of the verse, especially as it relates to Paul's strong ethical emphasis placed on humility and slavelike servanthood for all Christians who are united in the one Christian family (Eph 2:20-21; 3:7; 4:1-6, 25; 4:31—5:2; compare 1 Cor 7:22-24; Gal 5:13; Phil 2:1-11). Furthermore, when we view the broader textual context, the structure of Ephesians 5:18-21 indicates that mutual submission flows from being filled with the Spirit (v. 18). In the Greek, "be filled with the Spirit" is followed by the results of this infilling—speaking, singing, giving thanks—and servantlike submission is another listed consequence of the Spirit's presence in every believer's life.[20] In view of Paul's teaching on servantlike submission and in view of the Greek grammar of Ephesians 5:18-20, verse 21 is not to be minimized to reduce its tension with what follows.

Conversely, another approach is to take Ephesians 5:21 as an implied criticism of the hierarchical relationships that are mentioned next. In this approach, 5:21 is Paul's real view and the rest he simply debunks. This view takes seriously the force of 5:21, not only on its own but also its key location at the beginning of the passage, shaping what follows. Just as a bold heading in this chapter predisposes us to what we read in the subsequent section, so Ephesians 5:21 is thought to place what follows in a context of mutual submission. But this approach does not explain why Paul does not make this implied criticism clear in 5:22—6:8, when he gives the opposite impression of affirming these relationships. Furthermore, why would Paul give theological motivation for the wife's and husband's behavior in 5:23-27 when he does not really intend for this relationship to remain hierarchical?[21] The comparison of the relations of husband and wife with Christ and the church does not underscore mutual submission but "reinforces the cultural-patriarchal pattern of subordination, insofar as the relationship between Christ and the church clearly is not a relationship between equals, since the church-bride is totally dependent and subject to her head-bridegroom."[22]

These two alternatives, though irreconcilable, agree that the difference between Ephesians 5:21 and 5:22—6:8 creates a tension for us that we would prefer to resolve in some way. Apparently, however, Paul was able to keep the two parts together, as Elisabeth Schüssler Fiorenza rightly says, "The general injunction for all members of the Christian community, 'Be subject to one another in the fear of Christ,' is clearly spelled out for the Christian wife as requiring submission and inequality."[23] Of course, this last word of Fiorenza's (*inequality*) is a lapse back over to our side of the bridge, but her observation still stands. On Paul's side of the bridge it was possible for two to become "one in Christ" (Eph 4:1-4), just as they became "one flesh" through marriage (Eph 5:31; Gen 2:24). Yet a hierarchy exists so that the wife, the child and the slave remain subordinate to the husband, parent and master.

In Ephesians 5:33 Paul summarizes that the husband should love his wife but reminds her that she should deeply respect (or fear, *phobētai*) her husband. We will encounter this perplexing phenomenon again in the next chapter on slavery, where Paul apparently saw no contradiction between becoming spiritual siblings and remaining in a hierarchical master-slave relationship (for example, 1 Tim 6:2; Philemon). The egalitarian salvation that Christ has brought to men and women, slaves and masters, Jews and Greeks (1 Cor 12:13; Gal 3:28; Eph 5:21) works itself out by *beginning* to transform the way husbands and wives relate, but this high ideal is only to be worked out most fully much later. Even so, Paul himself sounds a call that inspires us to transcend the cultural limitations placed on his followers as we more fully appropriate Paul's right vision of social equality in Christ.[24]

In both Colossians and Ephesians, Paul balances his exhortation by addressing both wives and husbands as moral agents, giving us further inspiration to view the marital relationship in more egalitarian terms than Paul's contemporaries may have. Wives are to choose to be subject to their husbands as a result of their Christian discipleship (Eph 5:21-24; Col 3:18), and husbands are to cast off their socially granted right to be superior and harsh as they tenderly love their wives (Col 3:19).[25] This instruction is considerably expanded in Ephesians by comparing the husband's marital care of his wife with Christ's self-giving love for the church. To love one's wife is to love oneself, since the two have become one flesh.

One married woman I know commented to me, "I know a few men around who could do with reading this and applying it. I think it's hard for some women to respect and honor their husbands when their husbands don't love them in the way Paul is prescribing." Too true. Even though Paul leaves a husband's authority unquestioned, he sharply limits a husband's use of his authority by prescribing that it should mirror Christ's use of his own lordly authority, washing feet like a lowly slave (Jn 13), giving himself up in self-sacrificial love for the church. In this, Paul challenges the husband with the countercultural message of the gospel.

Consequently, if a husband's love is to be slavelike and sacrificial, then Paul's conservative view of the wife's role is not that much different from his broader vision for the Christian community, which includes husbands, parents and masters. Paul encourages wives to be subordinate in a very conservative Greco-Roman way, but this is the same model that he sets even for himself in his apostolic leadership when he identifies himself as a "slave of Christ" (Gal 1:10 my translation; compare 1 Cor 9:19-23; 2 Cor 4:5). This is the same role of subservience and obedience he envisions for all Christians (1 Cor 7:22; Phil

2:1-11). That is not to minimize Paul's hierarchical view of social relationships between wives and husbands but rather to locate those views within a broader framework of his thought, where service, humility, obedience and self-sacrifice are highly esteemed for *both* men and women. This must partly explain why Christianity was so popular among women and slaves of his day and softens the chauvinist timbre of these verses.

How then do we take Paul's perplexing mix of egalitarianism and hierarchy across to our side of the interpretive bridge? Some points transfer rather easily:

1. Mutual submission is the high calling of all Christian relationships.
2. Dominating and harsh uses of authority are ruled out.
3. Leadership is to be servantlike, tender and caring.
4. How I treat others affects me directly, because my wife and I are "one flesh" and other believers and I belong to one body in Christ.

More difficult for some readers—but clear to me—is the need for us to carry forward Paul's egalitarian vision of 1 Corinthians 12:13, Galatians 3:28 and Ephesians 5:21. These clear and noble notes need to be worked out more thoroughly than Paul may have worked them out. We should take Paul's vision of unity and equality in Christ into our views of how we relate to one another and order our lives. Some readers might object that this is an inappropriate use of the interpretive bridge, but I counter with three observations:

1. We translate other cultural conventions of the Bible quite easily and without any qualms. The holy kiss, head-coverings for prayer and foot washing are all commanded in the Bible, but we acknowledge that the principles underlying these commands can and should be translated to our new setting without our actually kissing each other in church, covering heads to pray or stripping off one another's shoes to fulfill Christ's command to serve each other. Obviously, we can embody in flexible ways the principles of gracious greeting, regard for another's conscience and a servant lifestyle. Changing cultures invite us to materialize these important Christian values in new forms that make sense in our setting, ways that may not have made sense on Paul's side of the bridge but cannot be sidestepped on our side.

2. If we were now discussing slavery instead of marriage, this methodology

would not be questioned. As Craig Keener candidly says, "Those who today will admit that slavery is wrong but still maintain that husbands must have authority over their wives are inconsistent."[26] That is, in both Ephesians and Colossians Paul affirms master-slave relationships at the same time as he discusses husbands and wives. (In the next chapter we discuss at length the issue of slavery.) The same interpretive filter that applies to slavery applies to marriage, though there are still principles that are to be derived from these passages. For example, mutual submission and the servant life are to be abiding Christian hallmarks.

3. Paul himself, in the three verses just cited (1 Cor 12:13; Gal 3:28; Eph 5:21), inspires us to anticipate and actualize a more thorough application of his Christ-given, egalitarian program than his followers may have. It is noteworthy that Paul invites us to build on what earlier Christians have accomplished (1 Cor 3:5-15), and we are encouraged to work out our salvation as fully as we can in our new cultural climate.

Some readers may feel tempted by the nostalgic tendency to idealize the past, remembering the "good ol' days" when Western society mirrored the hierarchy of the Greco-Roman world that finds expression in Paul's letters. These better times never existed for slaves or for women. It is positively unchristian to pine for a return to Victorian values and times, days where sexism was particularly distasteful, as characterized by the nineteenth-century expression, "Prostitutes for pleasure, concubines for service, wives for breeding."[27] That is not the affirmation of highly capable and industrious women that Paul inherited from Proverbs 31, and he gives us every reason to hope for much more from our relationships.

Paul's Celebration of the Single Life

Much attention naturally falls on Paul's thoughts about marriage, but he fares far better when we consider the timely, positive esteem he lavishes on the lifestyle choice of single adults. Paul himself was single, a station that he celebrated as a gift from God and a lifestyle that he urged on his followers. As a single adult, Paul lived a lifestyle that a rapidly growing number of adults are choosing today. Over the past twenty years, the number of American adults remaining single has doubled from twenty-one to forty-one million, accounting for 23 percent of all adults. In the same period, single-parent households have tripled. When one adds to these facts the observation that 60 percent of first-time marriages now end in divorce, we realize how much Paul as a single man has in common with a large and growing segment of the adult population in America.[28] In fact, Paul's view on singleness is evidence in favor of the apostle's relevance and timeliness in a day when so many of his views are simply dismissed without further thought.

Though Paul's high esteem of the single life may make him easy to relate to for growing numbers of single adults, some readers think that Paul's celebration of singleness alienated him from the culture of his time. Hyam Maccoby, for example, thinks that his singleness is the least Jewish thing about Paul and says of his teaching in 1 Corinthians 7:1-11,

> Nothing of this is derived from Judaism. Unmarried people, in Jewish tradition, are regarded with pity, not admiration. It was regarded as a duty to marry. Rabbis were all expected to be married, and the few exceptions were regarded as lacking in full humanity. Paul's reference to a "gift" of chastity would be regarded as unintelligible.[29]

This comment underlines the point made in the last chapter about the high view of marriage in aspects of ancient Judaism, but Maccoby overlooks some important pieces of *Jewish* evidence, of which three examples are given.

First of all, Jesus was apparently single, but this did not stop the masses from following him. Large numbers of Palestinian Jews did not view him to be lacking in full humanity; rather, they placed great hope in his superiority to the rabbis of their day. Second, in the Hebrew Scriptures, Jeremiah was called by God to singleness: "The word of the LORD came to me: You shall not take a wife" (Jer 16:1-2). Though Jeremiah's reasons are different from Paul's (compare Jer 16:4 and 1 Cor 7:26-35), Jeremiah the Jewish prophet shares with Paul the Jewish-Christian apostle a commitment to singleness as part of God's calling on his life.[30] Third, the Jewish community at Qumran (of Dead Sea Scrolls fame) practiced celibacy in Paul's time. Their views were not unknown in Palestine, and there are points of contact between Paul's letters and some of their distinctive beliefs.[31] It is not accurate to say that

Paul's views on singleness are un-Jewish.

When we consider that Paul was a Hellenistic Jew-become-Christian and that his teaching in 1 Corinthians 7 is addressed to a Greco-Roman congregation, we have to realize that, from their perspective, Paul's views on the single life would not have sounded completely alien. Epictetus, another Greco-Roman writer born toward the end of Paul's life, gives a long description of the popular philosophers known as Cynics. They prized the single life since they were to pursue their mission to the world like solders, eschewing material possessions and bodily pleasure in pursuit of detached contentment: "I sleep on the ground; I have neither wife nor children, no miserable governor's mansion, but only earth, and sky, and one rough cloak."[32]

Like the Cynics and not unlike Jesus, Jeremiah and the Essenes, Paul's celebration of celibacy would not have been unfamiliar. Even so, his own formulation of the importance of singleness is just as countercultural as theirs was. Although Paul is careful not to diminish the value of marriage, he asserts his own personal example of a lifestyle that bucked the dominant trend: "I wish that all were as I myself am. But each has a particular gift from God, one having one kind and another a different kind. To the unmarried and the widows I say that it is well for them to remain unmarried as I am" (1 Cor 7:7-8). There are several startling and positive affirmations of singleness in 1 Corinthians 7 that deserve comment.

First, Paul identifies singleness along with marriage as a "gift from God." The word for *gift* that he uses to describe the single lifestyle *(charisma)* is the same word he applies to the work that the Spirit of God accomplishes in the community through the God-endowed abilities of individual believers, such as the utterance of wisdom, the utterance of knowledge, faith, healing, miracles, prophecy, tongues, leadership and teaching (1 Cor 12:7-11, 28-31; Rom 12:6-8). It is especially noteworthy that Paul identifies the single life as a *charisma,* the same label he uses to characterize the free gift of salvation and eternal life (Rom 5:15-16; 6:23), the election and calling of Israel (Rom 11:29), a remarkable answer to prayer (2 Cor 1:11) and his own high status as an apostle (1 Cor 12:28; compare Gal 1:15). In a society where marriage was the presumed thing to do, Paul dignifies the minority single status by drawing attention to its equal standing with marriage as God-given.

This message is equally relevant today, when many single adults feel the pain of patronizing remarks, cutting questions about their desirability and the sting of suspicion about their sexuality. Such barbs give single people the impression that one is less than a whole number. In spite of the dramatic demographic trends toward singleness and single parenting, we still live in a society where normal is married-with-children. Paul sides with the single adult on this score, extolling the unmarried life without children.

Paul praises singleness in a second way, drawing attention to how the self-controlled single adult is in a better position to serve the Lord than the married person, whose loyalties are divided between ministry and family. Paul's reasoning is known and recognized by both ancients and moderns. In antiquity, the Cynics used the argument of the dispersed energies of a married person as a defense of the Cynic ideal of celibacy.[33] Many career-minded singles are devoted to their careers and acknowledge that as one reason some do not marry: "I can't get married. When would I have the time?" Career-minded singles, ancient popular philosophers and scripturally faithful Catholic priests acknowledge the practcal sense of Paul's advice:

> I want you to be free from anxieties. The unmarried man is anxious about the affairs of the Lord, how to please the Lord; but the married man is anxious about the affairs of the world, how to please his wife, and his interests are divided. And the unmarried woman and the virgin are anxious about the affairs of the Lord, so that they may be holy in body and spirit; but the married woman is anxious about the affairs of the world, how to please her husband. I say this for your own benefit, not to put any restraint upon you, but to promote good order and unhindered devotion to the Lord. (1 Cor 7:32-35)

Married life has many benefits, and Paul goes out of his way to affirm the goodness of marriage in this chapter (compare 1 Cor 6:15-16; Eph 5:31). Nevertheless, anyone who has been married has learned that a growing and healthy marriage requires time, energy, concessions and surrender of a considerable degree of autonomy—and more of these are required if children arrive on the scene. It is common for married clergy to feel pulled between the pressures of family life and the demands of their ministerial duties, and many a minister's spouse and children have known the dark side of these pressures. It is not that these two good things, marriage and ministry, are intrinsically opposed to each other. It is just that one person has only so much time and only so much energy, and Paul asserts—rightly I think—that remaining unmarried has the advantage of leaving one "unhindered" in the highest calling of "devotion to the Lord," whatever disadvantages there also may be.[34]

A third affirmation of the single life may be implied here too. By lifting the single life to an equally gifted status with marriage by both his teaching and personal example, there may be a social dynamic of liberation going on in 1 Corinthians that is often overlooked. In Greco-Roman society, usually only married men were granted the right to lead and govern in social clubs, religious societies and civic affairs. It may well be that just as Paul recognized women's leadership in reversal of the norm, so too he turns around the notion that one must be married to lead. Instead, he identifies both singleness and leadership as gifts of God and not the privilege of marital status or birth (compare 1 Cor 7:7; 12:28).

It has already been noted that he addresses single and married women alongside the men of the community (1 Cor 7:34). Thus, there may be an implied social critique and reversal going on in 1 Corinthians 7, in light of Christ's overarching social program that Paul explicitly announces early in the letter:

> Consider your own call, brothers and sisters: not many of you were wise by human standards, not many were powerful, not many were of noble birth. But God chose what is foolish in the world to shame the wise; God chose what is weak in the world to shame the strong; God chose what is low and despised in the world, things that are not, to reduce to nothing things that are, so that no one might boast in the presence of God. He is the source of your life in Christ Jesus, who became for us wisdom from God, and righteousness and sanctification and redemption, in order that, as it is written, "Let the one who boasts, boast in the Lord." (1 Cor 1:26-31)

It may well be that Paul's personal example of singleness as a leader and his commendation of this lifestyle to the women and men at Corinth are other instances of this social reversal principle of Christ's kingdom: God uses single leaders as another visible demonstration of God's power working through perceived human deficiencies. God is not limited by human biases, reversing the status of singles to show that "this all-surpassing power is from God and not from us," to borrow another phrase from Paul's conversation with the Corinthians (2 Cor 4:7 NIV).

Celibacy, the Coming Crisis and the Cosmic Clock

If Paul's views on celibacy and marriage are challenging enough at the brink of the twenty-first century, we encounter in his discussion of singleness an expectation of the end of history that merits its own consideration before concluding this chapter. Throughout 1 Corinthians 7 we can never forget that Paul is an ancient Christian apostle, fanatically committed to Christ, who has redeemed him, always reminding us of the brevity of time remaining on the historical clock. For the single, the married, the enslaved and the free he gives the conservative advice, "In whatever condition you were called, brothers and sisters, there remain with God" (1 Cor 7:24). If we take this sound bite out of its context, it would appear to reflect the view of a political conservative who was concerned about preserving things as they are, a morally question-able viewpoint to hold in an oppressive and unjust world. But this impression could not be further from the truth since Paul's reasoning is anything but calm and conservative:

> I think that, in view of the impending crisis, it is well for you to remain as you are. . . . I mean, brothers and sisters, the appointed time has grown short; from now on, let even those who have wives be as though they had none, and those who mourn as though they were not mourning, and those who rejoice as though they were not rejoicing, and those who buy as though they had no possessions, and those who deal with the world as though they had no dealings with it. For the present form of this world is passing away. (1 Cor 7:26, 29-31)

This reasoning for remaining single creates its own problems for understand-ing Paul, a tangent we now explore.

Paul has in mind that the stage is set for the end of world history, an ending that is impending and imminent. Paul envisions this final scene of the global drama in catastrophic and apocalyptic images of a coming crisis. It is a bleak view of the future, but it would not be accurate to call it pessimistic. The present world order is to pass away, but it is to be replaced with redeemed creation, renewed to its intended goodness and peace in the Creator's initial plan. In this renewed state of affairs, Christ will be truly worshiped as Lord of all (Phil 2:9-11). In this new order, the commonwealth of heaven will be ruled by the Sovereign Christ, who will transform our humble existence into an experience of this glorious and redeemed creation (Phil 3:20-21). Paul's short-term predictions are stark, but he sees the long-term prospects as very good indeed for those who submit to Christ as Lord.

Paul's apocalyptic vision of the end of the world and the return of Christ is no small part of his thought, and it is a common thread throughout the New Testament that extends back to the Old Testament prophets, who announced on God's behalf, "I am about to create new heavens and a new earth; the former things shall not be remembered or come to mind" (Is 65:17). Paul expresses eagerness for the return of Christ in the form of an Aramaic prayer, "Our Lord, come!" (*marana tha,* 1 Cor 16:22). This same thought is given expression elsewhere in Paul's letters (for example, 1 Thess 1:10; 5:2-3; 2 Thess 2:2-3; 2 Tim 3:1), a view that he shares with Jesus and the early Christians (Mark 13; Revelation). It is obvious that Paul, Jesus and the early church held to this things-will-get-far-worse-before-they-become-better-forever scheme of the future. If modern readers have trouble with this view of the end of the world, their problem is not just with Paul but with many of the writers of the New Testament.

Nevertheless, what do we make of Paul's comments about the shortness of time twenty centuries later? Time is so short, in Paul's view, that things may come to a head in the Corinthians' lifetime. How else can we explain his use of this as an additional motivation for their remaining single? He clearly has this in mind, for his instructions are partly motivated by the desire to spare his readers "distress in this life" (1 Cor 7:28). As he says in 1 Thessalonians, the Lord can return at any moment, "like a thief in the night," suddenly, and "there will be no escape" (1 Thess 5:2-4). As we look back with our 20/20 hindsight, we can see that time was not as short as Paul suspected. We face this fact when we view Paul's words from the vantage point of twenty additional centuries of human drama.

Paul's letters show that, already in his lifetime, Christians—and he himself—were wrestling with the problem of the delayed coming of Christ. In 2 Thessalonians he has to remind them that the imminent coming of Christ should not keep them from their practical affairs. Apparently, some had interpreted Christ's imminent return as reason to declare a permanent vacation from manual labor, a point Paul counters in strong terms (2 Thess 3:6-13). The return of Christ does not justify the neglect of daily duties, and, after all, Paul reminds them, the return of Christ comes after a period where signs of the end are revealed through catastrophic calamities (2 Thess 2:3-6).

These caveats in 2 Thessalonians should lead us to a reevaluation of his remarks about singleness in 1 Corinthians 7. Apparently, it is not merely the ticking clock that is Paul's reason for remaining single. Rather, Paul contemplates the cost to the married that the end-time suffering will bring. It is not merely that the end is *impending* but that it will bring with it a *crisis*. The coming closure of world history first brings anguish, birth pangs that signal the end. Jesus, like Paul, warns of the difficulty this period will pose for family life:

> Woe to those who are pregnant and to those who are nursing infants in those days! Pray that your flight may not be in winter or on a sabbath. For at that time there will be great suffering, such as has not been from the beginning of the world until now, no, and never will be. (Mt 24:19-21)

Thus, Paul's instructions parallel the teaching of Jesus about the future of Planet Earth, and his views make sense in light of the approaching apocalypse. Though the number of days remaining was greater than Paul anticipated, his advice is congruent with a future hope and expectation that now is not all, and the best is yet to be.

The Helpfulness of Paul's Hesitancy
It may help to consider that 1 Corinthians 7 contains Paul's most overtly

tentative instructions about the Christian life. When he is confident that he has teaching from the Lord on a matter, he commands and exhorts in no uncertain terms, "not I but the Lord" (v. 10). But on the importance of remaining single, he claims, "This I say by way of concession, *not of command,*" and, "I *wish* that all were as I myself am" (vv. 6-7). Since he had no instruction of what to do about remaining married to unbelievers, he makes clear that he is improvising: "To the rest I say—I and not the Lord" (v. 12). He returns to the subject of celibacy a little later and concedes, "I have no command of the Lord" (v. 25). This does not mean, however, that he does not feel firmly about the advice he gives: "I give my opinion as one who by the Lord's mercy is trustworthy" (v. 25). This is Paul's personal judgment in the matter, but he reminds them that his thoughts are guided by the Holy Spirit, "and I think that I too have the Spirit of God" (v. 40). He is confident in what he asserts about the single life, but he leaves the door open for other viewpoints, a highly notable element of this text.

If we have trouble with Paul's views on marriage and singleness, he already invites other viewpoints to the conversation. His unique contribution to this discussion, as we have seen, is not his traditional stance on husbands and wives or even his countercultural stance on singleness. Paul's unique contribution is to draw attention to the fact that devotion to Christ is to deeply affect one's practical decision-making and unquestioned cultural conditioning. If his ancient readers could expect an unchallenged male hierarchy, Paul calls them to consider the humble service of others in the Christian community of loving mutual submission. If they could be confident in their authoritarian stance, he challenges them to discover the secret of the Christian life in self-sacrificial caring for, rather than controlling of, others. If they could be smug in their social status as married and male, he challenges them to accept the gifting of the Spirit on the single and female. In all of these, Christlike thinking is to be first and foremost, and devotion to Christ is to be front and center. If Paul's views on social ordering jar us as dusty and antiquated, his obvious devotion to Christ shines through from his ancient social context, inspiring us to embody Christian love and teaching in equally devoted ways in our context.

5

The Slave
of Christ
& the Slaves
of Antiquity

*T*he subject of slavery is repugnant and repulsive. Our minds immediately fill with images of people oppressed for selfish gain, heart-
broken mothers torn from their children and cruel punishment that
scorns justice. Sadly, slavery is not simply a subject of historical interest but
remains a pressing issue in our global village. Progress has been made in
modern times, but slavery was not officially abolished in Saudi Arabia until
1963, Mauritania until 1980 and Mississippi until 1995!

It was reported in December 1988 that slaves were being sold for forty-five
dollars in Sudan. In 1989 China launched a national campaign against the
abduction and sale of women and children, an initiative that suggests widespread occurrence of this tragic and cruel crime. In Shaanxi province two
thousand cases were reported in 1989, seven thousand cases in Sichuan in
1990. Elsewhere in 1990, teenagers in Mozambique were reported as being
sold into slavery in South Africa. (Virtual slavery conditions also exist. For

example, six-year-old boys in Sialkot, Pakistan, are paid twenty rupees [sixty cents] for the four to five hours it takes to hand-stitch a soccer ball.)[1]

Against the backdrop of these human rights violations, we are stunned to read Paul's positive remarks about enslavement:

> Slaves, obey your earthly masters with fear and trembling, in singleness of heart, as you obey Christ; not only while being watched, and in order to please them, but as slaves of Christ, doing the will of God from the heart. Render service with enthusiasm, as to the Lord and not to men and women, knowing that whatever good we do, we will receive the same again from the Lord, whether we are slaves or free. (Eph 6:5-8)

This was not addressed to Chinese girls in 1990, but, if it were, we would regard it as utterly revolting and inexcusable. Adding to the assault on our contemporary sensibilities, Paul nowhere calls for an end to the slavery system. What possible explanation could there be for this oversight regarding a system we now view as flagrantly evil? A trip across the interpretive bridge is revealing.

Roman society and economics cannot be understood without grasping the centrality of slavery in their structure. As already suggested in the last chapter, slavery was considered as foundational to society as marriage and parenthood. Seldom did anyone in Paul's day reflect upon what was considered a normal part of Mediterranean life. No ancient government ever considered abolishing slavery. None of the slave rebellions, the last of which was 120 years before Paul's letters, aimed at abolishing slavery as an institution. (Revolts usually occurred among the ranks of gladiators or those enslaved for criminal punishment, who sought to reverse who was master and slave, not to put an end to slavery itself.) By Paul's time economic conditions had improved so much that slave uprisings were unheard of.

No key authors who had formerly been slaves attacked slavery as an institution, and no freed person championed slaves as a group.[2] The unquestioned acceptance of slavery in the ancient world explains why there are more than 190 words referring to slaves and slavery in the New Testament alone. The English reader may miss this obvious feature, since in our postslavery shame we have settled for the more benevolent English translation of "servant."[3]

Americans live with the constant shame and continuing legacy of New World chattel slavery. The estimated numbers are staggering and sickening. In the year 1790 alone, the British slave trade delivered an estimated seventy thousand souls into bondage to the Americas. During four hundred years of New World slavery, an estimated fifteen million people were purchased like cattle, and another forty million lost their lives in the notorious "middle passage"—the cruel transport of the kidnapped from their African homelands to the plantations of the Americas.

Slavery was a contributing cause to the bloodiest war in American history. The deep scar of the Civil War on our collective memory is marked by massive cemeteries, and the healing is not complete in a nation still rooting out the entrenched racism of those grim days. Although no voices are advocating a return to slavery in America, the shadow of those cruel centuries persists as more than memories. The rest of the world may have looked on in disbelief that the Los Angeles riots of the early 1990s could happen, but, though many Americans were shocked, they were not surprised. The fear and anger of those riots had long been raging beneath a thin veneer of civility.

Racial stereotyping, fear and hatred are a daily experience for much of America. It is not simply a problem on the fringes of society, involving extremists such as Skin Heads, the Ku Klux Klan and Louis Farrakhan. Widespread racial tensions along black-white lines are too prevalent, having their roots in the centuries-long color-conscious partitioning of society. These moral obscenities were only partly addressed by the Civil War and by the legal reforms of desegregation. Slavery is abolished, segregation and discrimination are illegal, but the scars and social habits bred in the soil of chattel slavery still linger.

Paul's letters have been bloodied by the Civil War, a fact that cannot be changed by softening the translation of "slave" with "servant." We have to admit that Paul's letters were the favorite texts to which American proslavery preachers turned most often to justify their position. We cannot escape this historical tragedy. These texts haunt us as they echo across the graves of dead slaves, maimed soldiers and assassinated civil rights leaders:

Were you a slave when called? Do not be concerned about it. . . . In whatever condition you were called, brothers and sisters, there remain with God. (1 Cor 7:21, 24)

Slaves, obey your earthly masters in everything, not only while being watched and in order to please them, but wholeheartedly, fearing the Lord. Whatever your task, put yourselves into it, as done for the Lord and not for your masters, since you know that from the Lord you will receive the inheritance as your reward; you serve the Lord Christ. For the wrongdoer will be paid back for whatever wrong has been done, and there is no partiality. (Col 3:22-25)

Let all who are under the yoke of slavery regard their masters as worthy of all honor, so that the name of God and the teaching may not be blasphemed. Those who have believing masters must not be disrespectful to them on the ground that they are members of the church; rather they must serve them all the more, since those who benefit by their service are believers and beloved. Teach and urge these duties. Whoever teaches otherwise and does not agree with the sound words of our Lord Jesus Christ and the teaching that is in accordance with godliness, is conceited, understanding nothing, and has a morbid craving for controversy and for disputes about words. (1 Tim 6:1-4)

Tell slaves to be submissive to their masters and to give satisfaction in every respect; they are not to talk back, not to pilfer, but to show complete and perfect fidelity, so that in everything they may be an ornament to the doctrine of God our Savior. (Tit 2:9-10)

These passages clearly tell slaves to be happy with their lot, because obedience to their masters displays Christlike behavior. Disobedience to a master (in the case of Col 3:25) is labeled as the same kind of sinful wrongdoing *(adikeō)* as sexual immorality, idolatry, adultery, homoeroticism, stealing and lying (1 Cor 6:8-10). When we realize that thousands of expository sermons were preached on these texts, sending many of the half-million Southern soldiers to their deaths confident that God was on their side, we are tempted to hold Paul accountable for the ways his letters were later used. We want to find Paul saying to Christian masters, "Free your slaves." Instead, we hear the opposite message when he says to slaves, "Be content in your bondage." What the

Abolitionists would have given for a single statement in Paul that echoed Moses' heart-cry for his enslaved people: "Let my people go" (Ex 5:1). Sadly, the pages of Paul contain nothing like this.[4]

How do we come to grips with this characteristic of Paul's letters, with what might appear to be their most morally reprehensible feature? First, we must acknowledge that the slave system Paul faced was significantly different from New World slavery. Second, we must give Paul credit for identifying with slaves, viewing himself as "a slave of Christ." Third, it is essential to realize that Paul regarded the spiritual human condition of all people as enslavement. For Paul, slavery to Christ is a shift of masters from sin to a savior, and the only path to true spiritual emancipation. Fourth, there is a liberating tendency in Paul's letters, and this must be given due recognition, as in the case of his attitude toward women. We must note that slaves, along with women, found Christianity very attractive. When we realize this, we must revise our initial, postmodern perception of how Paul's letters would have been heard and received. Finally, we should examine Paul's intervention on behalf of the slave Onesimus with his master Philemon to complete our understanding of Paul's views on slavery. These five considerations should alter our twentieth-century impression of Paul's attitude toward slavery.

1. The Differences Between Slavery in Antiquity and in America

Paul did not witness American chattel slavery. One of the most common interpretive mistakes is to assume that the Roman slavery Paul experienced was identical to the oppressive American system. Unlike the somewhat uniform agrarian and household subjugation of Negro slaves of the American South, Roman slavery is characterized best by its inability to be reduced to a single practice. As S. Scott Bartchy concludes in his lucid study of the subject, a person's experience in Roman slavery "depended almost entirely upon the customs of the owner's family, the business and the particular class of society to which the owner belonged, and the character of the owner himself."[5] This experience could vary dramatically, but in no way can Roman slavery be reduced to the subjugation and oppression experienced in America.

For example, it was illegal in the New World to teach slaves to read, but slaves in antiquity could be well educated. In one case, Marcus Tullius Cicero freed his slave Tiro, a slave of immense talent and education. Cicero's brother comments about it in a letter written about 53 B.C.E.:

> My dear Marcus, with regard to Tiro, I swear by my hope to see you, and my son Cicero, and little Tullia, and your son, that you gave me the very greatest pleasure when you decided that he, who did not deserve his bad fortune, should be our friend rather than our slave. Believe me, when I finished reading your letter and his,[6] I jumped for joy. And now I both thank you and congratulate you. For if Statius's faithful service brings such great pleasure to me, of what great value should these same fine qualities be in Tiro, especially when we take into account his literary skills, his conversational abilities, and his breadth of knowledge, qualities which are more significant than his ability to perform personal services for us.[7]

Tiro's literary skills must have been acquired through formal education, a far cry from the oppressive conditions that kept New World slaves illiterate. Cicero employed Tiro after his manumission (release from slavery) as a personal secretary and trusted confidant.

There was a wide range of experience in Roman slavery, but generally city slaves had a much more desirable and easy life than rural slaves. In a discussion on how to choose and deploy slaves for agrarian work, Columella details the differences between slave work in the city and in the country:

> A landowner must be concerned about what responsibility it is best to give each slave and what sort of work to assign to each. I advise that you not appoint a foreman from that type of slave who is physically attractive, and certainly not from the type who has been employed in the city, where all skills are directed toward increasing pleasure. This lazy and sleepy type of slave is accustomed to having a lot of time on his hands, to lounging around the Campus Martius, the Circus Maximus, the theaters, the gambling dens, the snack bars, and the brothels, and he is always dreaming of these same foolish pleasures. If a city slave continues to daydream when has been transferred to a farm, the landowner suffers the loss not just ˈlave but actually of his whole estate. You should therefore choose ˈo has been hardened to farm work from infancy, and who has

been tested by experience.[8]

Obviously, city slaves had an easier life than farm slaves, but farms slaves had it far better than those unfortunate souls consigned to the ranks of gladiators, prostitution or the mines. All this suggests a social setting rather different from the American South. But Roman slavery was not a benevolent institution. Some Roman slaves, particularly those who worked the mines or manned the oars, experienced dehumanizing and cruel conditions similar to those endured by Negro slaves in the American South, but most slaves in Roman mines or on galleys were there as punishment for criminal activities.

We must keep in mind the significant differences between Roman and American slavery when we consider Paul's apparent silence toward the slavery of his day. These differences could perhaps best be illustrated in a side-by-side comparison.

American Chattel Slavery	Ancient Greco-Roman Slavery
1. Slavery a permanent condition, a "life sentence" with no hope of freedom.	1. Unless a criminal, a slave had every hope of emancipation—usually a ten-to-twenty-year condition after reaching adulthood.
2. Slavery racially delineated: Negro slaves, white masters.	2. Impossible to distinguish a slave on the basis of color, clothing or race.
3. Slaves segregated socially.	3. Usually unable to distinguish a slave from others by friends, occupation or worship patterns. As a tentmaker Paul probably worked alongside slaves, who could join the same clubs as freed people and free people.
4. Slaves had no legal rights.	4. Slaves had many legal rights, including the right of appeal to a higher authority in the case of unfair treatment.

5. Slavery the lowest rung of society.

5. Slaves were often of higher status than the free, depending on who their masters were. A slave of Caesar, the largest slave owner by far, could command significant power and prestige.[9] From this high status, there was a continuum down to the very lowest rung of society.

6. Slavery was degrading and dehumanizing.

6. Slavery was viewed as an opportunity. Large numbers of persons sold themselves into slavery to find a better life than they had as free people and to secure special jobs and to climb socially.

7. Slaves confined to menial work.

7. Slaves held high positions in civil service and in the business world. Attended their owners as doctors and nurses, taught and advised their young owners and acted as companions and protectors to elderly owners. Were writers, accountants, bailiffs, overseers, secretaries and sea captains. For example, Marcus Antonius Felix, the Judean procurator who judged Paul (Acts 23:23—24:27), was a freed person of Claudius's mother, Antonia.

8. Illegal to educate slaves.

8. Slaves often highly educated, acting as tutors and advisers for their owners.

Slaves not able to own property.

9. Slaves could own property, could maintain savings for the day of their manumission and even owned their own slaves.

10. Slaves had no hope of normal family life.	10. Slaves often maintained a separate existence from their masters, even holding down outside work to increase their savings.
11. Slavery was wholly detestable, as a result of kidnapping.	11. Slavery was often preferred and chosen. Manumission was frequently a disadvantage for the slave and financially advantageous for the master.

The most important difference between the two is probably the first. Unlike New World slaves, Greco-Roman slaves could realistically expect faithful service to be rewarded with freedom and concomitant Roman citizenship, usually within ten to twenty years after achieving adulthood. At the turn of the millennium the numbers of slaves being freed was so large as to create social and political problems, so much so that emperors enacted laws to limit the number of slaves that could be freed by their masters. Augustus enacted a law requiring a slave to be at least thirty years old before manumission. As a law that was intended to reduce the flow of freed people, this suggests that slaves were often younger than thirty when they were set free. After the enactment of this law, the evidence shows that there still was a high rate of manumissions for those under age thirty, even among Caesar's own slaves![10]

It was to a master's financial advantage to free a slave under certain conditions, since the slave's accrued savings (called a *peculium*) would be paid to the master upon manumission, often worth far more than what the slave would sell for on the market. Also, the terms of freedom could be written in such a way as to obligate the ex-slave to continue specific services for the master. In return, the master benefited by no longer shouldering the burden of room and board for a full-grown adult. It is striking to note that at the time of Paul one-third of the population were slaves, but another one-third were former slaves! There was no equivalent practice of manumission for Negro slaves in the South. Freedom was obtained by risking one's life on the "un derground railroad" to the North and leaving one's family and friends behind.

A striking paradox developed in Greco-Roman society: it was not primarily slaves but free workers who were exploited. It was in the owner's best interest to take good care of a slave as a significant capital investment, but there was no such commitment to the welfare of workers. Epictetus, a former slave himself, cites the feelings of a freed person who even longed for his previous life in slavery: "Why, what was wrong with me? Someone else kept me in clothes and shoes, and supplied me with food, and nursed me when I was sick; I served him in only a few matters. But now, miserable man that I am, what suffering is mine, who am a slave to several instead of one."[11]

In the days of Paul the lot of Greco-Roman slaves was steadily improving through legal action and the pressure of public opinion. During this century there was increasing recognition that slaves were human beings and not simply financial investments. The Stoic Seneca the Younger wrote to his friend Lucilius,

> I was happy to learn from people who had just visited you that you live on friendly terms with your slaves. This attitude is quite in keeping with your good sense and your liberal education. Some people say, "They're just slaves." But they are fellow human beings! "They're just slaves." But they live with us! "They're just slaves." In fact, they are our fellow slaves, if you stop to consider that fate has as much control over us as it has over them.[12]

Seneca goes on to argue that masters should break free of the shackles of social rank by choosing to eat with and befriend their slaves and, by all means, avoiding cruelty to them. He plants the thought (reminiscent of 1 Cor 7:21-24) that it is possible to be a free person in spirit regardless of one's social condition. Furthermore, he argues, it is possible for masters to be in greater bondage than their slaves, since freedom is more a matter of character than possession of the right of self-determination. All of this suggests a rising

᠁ for the slaves of Paul's time.

᠁ the first two centuries of the Christian era, the tendency of Roman

᠁ to limit the master's power over the slave and to guarantee

᠁ of slaves. From the time of Christ forward, there was an

᠁ disapproval of ruthless laws and the arbitrary power of

masters. For example, both Seneca and Dio Cassius report the story of Vedius Pollio: Vedius became angry with a slave for breaking his crystal vase in front of guests, who included Augustus Caesar. Vedius commanded that the slave be thrown into his pond of flesh-eating eels. Augustus responded to the slave's cries for help by demanding that all Vedius's crystal be smashed and thrown into the pond in place of the slave.[13] This story illustrates both the capricious capacity of a master and the shifting Roman sensibilities as embodied by Augustus. The rights of slaves were increasing, and the responsibilities of masters toward their slaves increased accordingly. The improving legal, social and economic conditions and the real likelihood of emancipations probably account for the absence of slave unrest during Paul's lifetime.

When we read Paul's comments about slavery, we must keep in mind these improving conditions for slaves and that slavery was often temporary. Furthermore, we must remember that many of Paul's hearers had chosen the path of slavery as a means of social advancement. As much as we are able, we must cross over the interpretive bridge to Paul's world and put out of our minds recent North American slave systems, which were significantly different.

2. Paul, the Slave of Christ
Paul calls himself a "slave of Christ," his favorite way of describing both his missionary calling as an apostle and the Christian's relationship with Christ. In our environment of rigid political correctness, we might suppose that this shows that Paul was wholly insensitive to slaves of his day. It is our custom to excise from our speech references to social groups for fear of being labeled a hate monger. On the contrary, Paul's use of slave imagery could powerfully communicate because it identified with the slave experience of a significant majority of his readers.[14]

Paul was not putting down slaves as subhuman as many of his contemporaries had done; rather, he radically identified with those who were slaves, employing a principle of effective communication. In a society where two-thirds of the population had personal experience of slavery, one-third formerly and one-third presently, it is significant that Paul uses "slave of Christ" to point to his own servitude, obligation and devotion to Christ.[15]

We should pause to mention that the title *kyrios,* which our English Bibles often translate "Lord," would be heard in a slave economy as the common word for master. *Lord* usually has a spiritual connotation for us, but the same word in Greek could evoke social images of literal masters. Paul's emphasis on obedience to the "Lord" would be heard by many Greco-Roman readers as obedience to the "Master" Jesus, who had the legitimate right to control one's life and shape one's destiny, for he "bought [us] with a price" (1 Cor 6:20; 7:23), making us "freed person[s]" *(apeleutheroi)* ransomed by the Lord (1 Cor 7:22). So, for example, in 2 Corinthians 4:5 Paul contrasts Jesus as Lord/Master with his and his coworkers' role as "your slaves for Jesus' sake."

Paul places the self-description "slave of Christ" up front in several letters. He introduces himself to the Romans as "Paul, a slave of Jesus Christ, called to be an apostle, set apart for the gospel of God" (Rom 1:1 my translation). To the Philippians he identified himself with Timothy as the letter's senders: "Paul and Timothy, slaves of Christ Jesus" (Phil 1:1 my translation). In the introduction to Romans, both "slave of Christ" and "apostle" are used (compare Gal 1:1, 10; Tit 1:1), but in Philippians "slave of Christ" stands alone, when we usually find "apostle" added in the other letters. Paul understood his relationship to Christ as his Lord *(kyrios)* in terms of a slave's loyalty, submission and obedience to his master.[16] As Francis Lyall says, it is "clear that for Paul, 'the slave of Christ,' all his goods, time, ambitions, and purposes were subject to the determination of Christ. Paul was no different from an ordinary slave: he was at his Master's disposal."[17]

In Galatians, Paul again identifies himself as a slave of Christ (Gal 1:10) and portrays the relationship as one of exclusive loyalty to his master. The Galatians were facing pressure to submit to a different form of the Christian message, and throughout the letter Paul depicts their alternatives as choices between which master they will serve, either Christ or others, bringing a version of the gospel that required them to be circumcised (Gal 1:10; 2:3-5; 4:7, 26, 30-31; 5:1, 13). With slave-master imagery, Paul sets the scene for these alternatives: "Am I now seeking human approval, or God's approval? Or am I trying to please people? If I were still pleasing people, I would not be Christ's slave" (Gal 1:10 my translation). To please people is the choice to be a servile flatterer, enslaved to others rather than to Christ. The thrust of Galatians is to ensure that the readers will choose "God pleasing" and Paul's gospel. The alternative of submitting to Paul's opponents by accepting circumcision is characterized as submitting "again to a yoke of slavery" (Gal 5:1). In the face of this alternative master, Paul portrays himself in Galatians 1:10 as enslaved and loyal to Christ, a fidelity that grants him boldness and confidence to face down those who oppose Christ's free gift of grace (Gal 2:4-5), even if he must publicly confront Peter himself (vv. 11-14).[18]

When Paul identifies himself as a slave of Christ, he means that "Christ is my master, and I am controlled by no one and nothing else." As James Dunn says, "Paul implies, clearly, that his commitment to Christ as his Lord was so complete, his obligations to Christ so absolute, that his actions as an apostle of Christ were directed by him alone, and that any other course would be unthinkable for him."[19] But whereas literal, sociological slavery would have been the experience of two-thirds of Paul's readers and undoubtedly would have informed their reading of these metaphors, there are at least two other dimensions of the slave metaphor that should be kept in mind.

To all but the most upperclass readers, "Christ's slave" may have been perceived as a metaphor of power by affiliation with the most important person in the cosmos, much as a member of the *familia Caesaris* might claim his or her unique social status as Caesar's slave.[20] As a slave of Caesar held significant political power and social status because of whose they were, so Paul's identification with Christ as his slave may have carried similar connotations of authority and power-by-affiliation.

Also significant background for our understanding is the Old Testament usage of "slave of Yahweh" (Hebrew: *'ebed Yahweh;* Greek: *doulos kyriou*) for prestigious leaders such as Moses, Joshua, David and Isaiah.[21] For readers schooled in the Old Testament, this would also give the phrase "slave of Christ" a connotation of privilege and honor. There is reason to suspect that this use of "slave" in Jeremiah and Isaiah partly influenced Paul's usage in Galatians 1.[22]

Galatians 1:15-16 has at least three points of contact with Jeremiah 1:5 and Isaiah 49:1: (1) a commission for God's messenger, who is characterized as a "slave" who belongs to God;[23] (2) the assignment to this task from the womb of his mother; (3) the express instruction to go to the Gentiles. These features are suggestive that Paul might have identified himself in a way that echoes these Old Testament characterizations of God's messengers. The implication in Galatians 1, as in Jeremiah and Isaiah, is that on hearing the words of God's messenger one should not reject them. To reject the words of the messenger is to reject the divine sender.

We are not forced to choose between Greco-Roman and Old Testament backgrounds as we examine Paul's use of the slave-master metaphor. Paul himself uses "slave" as a metaphor with a wide range of flexibility, and the original readers would have heard the phrase with varying nuances. Specifically, he uses "slave" in a literal sense as a reference to sociological slavery (1 Cor 7; Philemon), as political rhetoric in the designation of a populist leader "enslaved" to his constituency (1 Cor 9:19-23; compare 2 Cor 4:5),[24] and theologically portraying the effects of sin (for example, Romans 6) or the benefits of redemption.[25] Likewise, the metaphor "slave of Christ" can have a multiple effect: characterizing Paul's leadership in terms of the Old Testament prophets to some; emphasizing the Christian life and apostolic service as the result of compulsion and subordination to most; but also hinting at Paul's power-by-affiliation with the most important person in the cosmos.

Paul continually uses various words for "slave" and "slavery" to describe his vocation as Christ's missionary.[26] For example, in 2 Corinthians 2:14 Paul plays on the image of the slave captured in war, a nuance lost in the English translation: "But thanks be to God, who in Christ always leads us in triumphal procession [thriambeuonti], and through us spreads in every place the fragrance that comes from knowing him."

The thriambolos was a slave seized by the conquering Roman army and paraded through the streets to display the glory of Rome and the inferiority and subjugation of the inhabitants of the newly annexed territory. In the centuries before Christ, this was the most common way one became a slave, and a majority of the slaves and freed people in Paul's churches were probably descendants of these prisoners of war. Peter Marshall has shown how this social setting and the context of 2 Corinthians inform us about Paul's use of the metaphor (compare 1 Cor 4:9-13; 2 Cor 4:7-12; 6:4-9). Paul is Christ's slave, who has been captured and enslaved (in reference to his dramatic turnabout on the Damascus road; see Acts 9), and now is paraded throughout the empire by God as a means of spreading the knowledge of Christ.[27] An awareness of this slave convention is essential for grasping the rhetorical impact of Paul's remark, imagery that would not be lost on those enslaved by capture in war, their descendants or the average Greco-Roman reader.

Another example of Paul's heavy reliance on slave imagery is in 1 Corinthians 9:16-23, where Paul again depicts his missionary service in language that both echoes the slave images of Jeremiah (20:9) and is grounded in common Greco-Roman slave metaphors. Paul preaches the gospel by compulsion, or "obligation" (*ananke*, v. 16, NKJV), a term that was commonly associated with slavery and subservience.[28] Thus, he is a missionary who does not expect a wage but involuntarily serves as a faithful, enslaved steward managing the household (v. 17). He has already introduced slavery as a metaphor for the Christian life in the letter (1 Cor 7:22), and now he uses the image to explain why he does not receive wages for his missionary labors even though he is entitled to them. By application he provides a model for how the Corinthians should give up their freedom to eat idol meat, the subject treated in 1 Corinthians 8 and 10.[29] In 9:19 he says, "For though I am free of all, I have enslaved *[edoulōsa]* myself to all of them in order that I may win the many" (my translation). In the same way, it is his hope that those who eat idol meat willingly will give up their freedom on behalf of those in the community whose consciences are offended.

The ways and means of Paul's missionary life demonstrate very tangibly that the metaphor "slave of Christ" is more than a figure of speech and has very practical, costly and even literal implications for Paul's life of servitude. This slavelike self-understanding is clearly stated in 2 Corinthians 4:5: "We do not preach ourselves but Jesus Christ as Lord, and ourselves as your slaves on account of Christ" (my translation). Paul presents himself as someone who identifies with the life of a slave, and it is no wonder that slaves found his message appealing. In Paul they found someone who understood them, identified with them and communicated the Christian life and message in concrete metaphors they could understand.

3. Slavery as Salvation

Paul goes beyond describing his own missionary life in slave imagery to depicting salvation for all Christians as redemption out of spiritual slavery: "You were bought at a price" (1 Cor 6:20; 7:23). As a Jewish convert to Christianity, Paul brought with him the rich remembrance of God's deliverance of the Israelites from slavery in Egypt. The annual remembrance of this rescue formed a central part of the worship calendar and Jewish identity. Every year at the Passover, the Jewish people remembered and celebrated their miraculous liberation from the hands of the pharaohs who had enslaved and oppressed them for more than four hundred years. This exodus was as critical to their corporate memory as was their origin from the faithfulness of Abraham and Sarah. God instructed Moses, as he interpreted this event for the future of Israel:

> Say therefore to the Israelites, "I am the LORD, and I will free you from the burdens of the Egyptians and deliver you from slavery to them. I will redeem you with an outstretched arm and with mighty acts of judgment. I will take you as my people, and I will be your God. You shall know that I am the LORD your God, who has freed you from the burdens of the Egyptians." (Ex 6:6-7)

After this had come to pass, the annual Passover celebration reenacted the details of these events to remember God's deliverance of their ancestors and their gratitude for God's mercy. As a nation and as a religion, redemption from slavery was crucial to their self-understanding. It is not surprising then that Paul adapts this theme to the Christian life, where the Christian is a "freed person" *(apeleutheros)* ransomed by the Lord (1 Cor 7:22-23; compare Lev 25:54-55). Whereas the Israelites had been delivered as a nation from literal, sociological slavery, so all those who belong to Christ have been delivered from the law of sin and death that held them in spiritual captivity.

Paul develops the imagery of salvation as God's redemption from slavery in two different ways. In Romans 8 and Galatians 4 he portrays salvation as God's adoption of slaves, making children out of those formerly indentured to sin and the law.[30] Differently, in Romans 6 he depicts salvation as a transfer of masters, from sin to God. In both images Paul builds his theological points around commonplace social experiences. It was common for a slave to be sold by one owner to another, sometimes as a result of the slave's protests about the cruelty of the previous master. Likewise, it was usual enough for a slave to be freed in order to be married or to be adopted by the former master. For example, on a tomb in Macedonia is an inscription commemorating a boy who had been born into slavery as the son of a slave but was later manumitted and adopted by his owner:

> Here lies Vitalis, first the slave, then the son of Gaius Lavius Faustus. I was born in his home as a slave. I lived sixteen years and I was a salesman in a shop. I was pleasant and well liked, but I was snatched away by the gods. I beg you, travelers and passers-by, if ever I shortchanged you to bring more profit to my father, please forgive me. And I beg you, by the gods above and below, that you treat my father and mother with kindness and respect. Farewell.[31]

In like manner Paul portrays the state of the Christian before baptism into Christ as one of bondage to sin and fear, and afterward as adoption as God's children:

> For you did not receive a spirit of slavery to fall back into fear, but you have received a spirit of adoption. When we cry, "Abba! Father!" it is that very Spirit bearing witness with our spirit that we are children of God, and if children, then heirs, heirs of God and joint heirs with Christ. (Rom 8:15-17)

Slavery is a metaphor for our spiritual state, characterized as a "spirit of slavery," before Christ's work. What Vitalis experienced as a literal slave adopted by his master-become-father we experience when the Spirit of God indwells us, assuring us of our "adoption" as children, encouraging us to cry out to God, "Dear Father." This imagery underlies Galatians 4 as well. Before our redemption by Christ we were slaves of "the elemental spirits of the world" (v. 3). God's sending of Jesus has "redeemed" us, that is, paid our emancipation price, "so that we might receive adoption as children" (v. 5; compare 1 Cor 6:20; 7:23). Paul concludes,

And because you are children, God has sent the Spirit of his Son into our hearts, crying, "Abba! Father!" So you are no longer a slave but a child, and if a child then also an heir, through God. Formerly, when you did not know God, you were enslaved to beings that by nature are not gods. (Gal 4:6-8)

In Romans 6 Paul uses slavery metaphors again, though differently from Romans 8 and Galatians 4. In Romans 6 he portrays life for all people as slavery, where each of us chooses one of two masters, "either of sin, which leads to death, or of obedience, which leads to righteousness" (v. 16). Those who have been baptized have been redeemed from "sin" as their "master," but they trade masters when they become Christians, since they "have become slaves of righteousness" (v. 18). Paul often exhorts his readers to become more of what they already are. Here he urges the Romans in this same manner. Even though they are already "slaves of righteousness," redeemed at the price of the life of God's dear son, they are to become more of what they are, devoting themselves to the things that please God:

For just as you once presented your members as slaves to impurity and to greater and greater iniquity, so now present your members as slaves to righteousness for sanctification. When you were slaves of sin, you were free in regard to righteousness. . . . But now that you have been freed from sin and enslaved to God, the advantage you get is sanctification. The end is eternal life. For the wages of sin is death, but the free gift of God is eternal life in Christ Jesus our Lord. (Rom 6:19-20, 22-23)

Spiritual slavery, in Paul's view, is the greatest evil and enemy of human happiness. It is possible to be a master, sociologically speaking, and remain a spiritual slave. Likewise, it is possible to be a literal slave but experience spiritual liberty through faith in Christ. Although Paul did not confront the political aspects of slavery, he confronted the larger—and in his view more significant—issue of one's relationship with God and one's need to be freed from the bondage of sin. In so doing, he presented both his missionary call and the elements of his gospel in terms that drew upon the day-to-day lives of his followers, metaphors that would be recognizable whether one was a slave, freed person or master.

This aspect of Paul's self-portrayal and missionary teaching grounded his message in the real-life experience of his readers and improved the effectiveness of his letters as communiqués, since all communication relies upon identification. The days of the slave economy are gone, but personal and social spiritual bondage remain an issue in our global village, where addiction, insurmountable social evils and personal cruelties have plumbed new lows. Paul's message of liberty for the human soul that comes through Jesus Christ remains timely and important, even as we are glad that the social condition of slavery has mostly disappeared from our planet.

4. The Liberating Tendency in Paul
It would be naive to fault Paul for not making an all-out frontal assault on the institution of slavery. What would a meaningful protest have meant in a stratified society where there were no referenda, no public opinion surveys, no democratic process for the masses? Furthermore, a protest against slavery as such would have been interpreted as treason and sedition since, as already mentioned above, slavery (along with marriage and family) was viewed as one of the basic building blocks of the city and the empire. If Paul had protested against slavery, his protests would surely have been reason for his imprisonment, trial, punishment and even execution. The Roman political-military machine was ruthless in putting down protests, and its *Pax Romana* ("the Roman Peace"), although characterized by an absence of war, was not accompanied by a democratization of society. It probably never occurred to Paul to lodge such a protest, and it is anachronistic for us to fault him from our social-legal position that cherishes the right of free speech. On Paul's side of the interpretive bridge, such rights did not exist, and those who dismiss him for his quietism on slavery have not grasped the tenuous position of an individual or fledgling church in the face of Roman might.

We should not be surprised that Paul does not lodge a forthright protest against Roman law and society, but we are urged to seek to answer a question whose answer is revealing about how Paul was perceived by slaves on his side of the interpretive bridge: Why did slaves find the Christian message so appealing?

It is a striking feature that one-fourth of the New Testament letters explicitly deal with the issue of slaves and masters in the Christian community: 1 Corinthians, Ephesians, Colossians, 1 Timothy, Titus, Philemon and 1 Peter. Notably, all but one of these are Pauline letters, indicating the appeal that Paul's teaching had to slaves. There was something about Christianity that caused slaves to be drawn into the proliferating house churches, a trend that continued through the first centuries of the early church.[32] This historical phenomenon gives us reason to examine closely Paul's letters to see if we can discover the same liberating tendency toward slaves as we found toward women. Since slaves found the Christian message to be appealing, we should expect to find in Paul's letters an attitude that slaves of his day would hear as releasing and positive.

First, we must consider the programmatic passages, which include slaves along with masters in the one new humanity incorporated into the church. Baptism into Christ and the church is the great equalizer in Paul's liberating gospel:

> For by one Spirit we were all baptized into one body, whether Jew or Hellene, whether slaves or free, and all drink of one Spirit. (1 Cor 12:13, my translation)
>
> There is no longer Jew or Greek, there is no longer slave or free, there is no longer male and female; for all of you are one in Christ Jesus. (Gal 3:28)
>
> In that renewal there is no longer Greek and Jew, circumcised and uncircumcised, barbarian, Scythian, slave and free; but Christ is all and in all! (Col 3:11)

In these passages Paul sows the seeds for the "tactful revolution of the new age," as Robert Jewett has memorably put it.[33] Although Paul does not work out this spiritual unity accomplished in baptism into a social policy that eliminates the slave institution (compare Col 3:11 with 3:22—4:1), he sounds the blast for a social revolution, and we must credit him for sounding the charge.

A second indication of the liberating tendency in Paul may be found in the household codes of Ephesians 6 and Colossians 3. It is striking to note who Paul addresses first in each pair of relationships: wives before husbands, children before parents and slaves before masters. Paul accomplishes a social reversal by addressing the supposed inferior members first. Not only does he call them equally saved in Christ, but he writes to them as though their social status does not prevent them from being addressed as equal members of the church. If society thought of slaves as property, Paul addressed them as people. If the law required obedience, Paul makes the life of slavery into an act of devotion, where service to Christ is the highest good.

Likewise, Paul encourages masters to work out their relationship with their slaves in ways that tangibly demonstrate their equality in Christ. They are to apply the Golden Rule to their treatment of slaves: "Masters, treat your slaves justly and fairly, for you know that you also have a Master in heaven" (Col 4:1). Since the Lord is the master of all masters and slaves, slave-holders should remain aware "that whatever good we do, we will receive the same again from the Lord, whether we are slaves or free" (Eph 6:8). Masters, therefore, should not intimidate their slaves, since "both of you have the same Master in heaven, and with him there is no partiality" (v. 9). James Bailey and Lyle Vander Broek conclude in their treatment of these domestic codes, "Although this code may sound crudely patriarchal to us, in light of its setting in a Hellenistic world in which the household head had absolute power over his subordinates, this Christianizing of the form surely represents a liberating tendency."[34]

A third indication of the liberating tendency in Paul can be found in the way he treats slavery as somewhat of an exception in his line of argument in 1 Corinthians 7. The main thrust of his exhortation is that everyone should be content in their current social condition, whether single or married (v. 27), circumcised or uncircumcised (vv. 18-19), slave or free (vv. 21-23). In the statements on both sides of his comments to slaves, Paul reiterates that whatever condition one was in when one became a Christian, there they should be content to remain (vv. 21, 24). Slaves are the only exception to this general principle, since they would have no choice if their master chose to manumit them. Therefore, Paul tells them, if they must remain slaves, "Don't worry about it. But, if you are also able to be freed, rather make use of [your freedom]" (v. 21 Bartchy's translation).[35] The social reality was that slaves could be—and often were—emancipated. Paul anticipates this occasion by encouraging them to use their freedom to serve the Lord as his slaves (v. 22). In addition, we get a hint that Paul was against the common practice of selling oneself into slavery: "You were bought with a price; do not become slaves of human masters" (v. 23).

The liberating tendency, the seeds of the tactful revolution of the new age of Christ's kingdom, are present throughout Paul's letters. In several places he announces the spiritual equality that slaves possess with their masters. Slaves must have taken him very seriously on this point, since they must be corrected:

> Let all who are under the yoke of slavery regard their masters as worthy of all honor, so that the name of God and the teaching may not be blasphemed. Those who have believing masters must not be disrespectful to them on the ground that they are members of the church; rather they must serve them all the more, since those who benefit by their service are believers and beloved. Teach and urge these duties. (1 Tim 6:1-2)

This correction would not have been needed unless slaves were interpreting Paul's message literally. Elsewhere, Paul begins to work out their unity in Christ in ways that value the slaves and inhibit masters' domination. Positively, he anticipates emancipations and counsels against self-sale into slavery.

The most profound expression of Paul's liberating tendency toward slaves and slavery can be seen in his intervention on behalf of the slave Onesimus with his master Philemon:

> Perhaps this is the reason he was separated from you for a while, so that you might have him back forever, no longer as a slave but more than a slave, a beloved brother—especially to me but how much more to you, both in the flesh and in the Lord. So if you consider me your partner, welcome him as you would welcome me. . . . Confident of your obedience, I am writing to you, knowing that you will do even more than I say. (Philem 15-17, 21)

5. The Case of Philemon and His Slave Onesimus

The letter of Philemon, like other letters, implies a story that must be inferred from the text and reconstructed within the possibilities that the social context permits. The implied story behind Philemon begins with Philemon incurring a debt to Paul (v. 19) and ends with Paul's anticipated arrival at Philemon's house (v. 22). Between these two ends, Philemon's slave Onesimus comes to Paul, and Paul writes a letter to influence favorably Philemon's reception of his slave.[36]

The traditional explanation for why Onesimus came to Paul is that he was a runaway,[37] but the recent adaptation of this view by Peter Lampe, S. Scott Bartchy and Brian Rapske is more likely: Onesimus sought a third party his master respected (an *amicus domini*) to become his advocate before his aggrieved owner, a common case in Roman legal evidence and thus referred to in verse 15.[38] The latter option is preferred because the traditional view suffers from crucial flaws in its various presentations. If Onesimus was simply an imprisoned runaway, the authorities were legally obliged to return him or the proceeds from his sale to his master. Or, if Onesimus were not in prison with Paul, it is difficult to imagine why Onesimus would seek the company of a friend of his master if he were seeking to disappear, why Onesimus as a runaway was permitted by the authorities to visit Paul who was under their guard[39] (a location not recognizable as a place of asylum[40]) and why Paul could feel free to send him back to Philemon (v. 12).

The elements of Philemon make better sense if Onesimus's goal was not to run away successfully but rather to return to his owner's household under improved conditions, a strategy that would not make him a fugitive.[41] He sought Paul to adjudicate a grievance he had with his master precisely because he knew Philemon respected Paul. The whole case may revolve around Onesimus's wrongdoing ("If he has wronged you," v. 18). While he was with Paul, Onesimus converted to Christ (vv. 10-11, 15-16), and the combination of Onesimus's new Christian status and Paul's previous relationship with Philemon forms the basis of Paul's appeal to Philemon.[42]

Paul begins his entreaty in verse 8 only to qualify continually his petition until it is finally stated in verse 17: Paul asks Philemon to receive Onesimus back with favorable regard (compare vv. 10-12, 17),[43] acting in a way that is congruent with love (vv. 5, 7; compare vv. 1, 9, 16).[44] The specifics of this directive are not detailed, and equally unspecified are "your duty" (v. 8; compare "out of place," Eph 5:4; "as is fitting," Col 3:18), "your good deed" (v. 14) and what things will fill Paul with joy and refresh him "in Christ" (v. 20). Presumably, Philemon would recognize what his obligations were. If Onesimus's wrongdoing was the impetus for his seeking out Paul as his advocate then Paul's appeal, without mentioning it, is that Philemon will put aside his somewhat justified anger and be reconciled to his slave. Paul does not overlook the financial loss that Philemon has incurred by the absence of his slave Onesimus (and perhaps by his wrongdoing), but in good rhetorical fashion he deflects a potential objection by promising to make recompense to Philemon (vv. 18-19), which the law would have required of him if he had harbored Onesimus as a runaway.[45]

Onesimus has become one of them as their "brother" (v. 16), thus becoming a partner of their shared service to Christ. Not only is he Paul's disciple ("child," v. 10) and "very heart" (v. 12), but vicariously he carries on Philemon's ministry (v. 13). Thus, the partnership that is portrayed in egalitarian relief is leveraged to full effect for Onesimus's benefit. When Paul asks Philemon to receive Onesimus "as you would receive me," he means that Philemon should give Onesimus full acceptance as a one of those who shares in the work of the family of Christ (compare Rom 15:7).[46] Furthermore, there may be an implied admonishment: "If you do not receive Onesimus as you would receive me, you will prove to me that you are neither my partner nor a brother."[47] The cumulative dynamics of the letter encourage Philemon to extend to Onesimus the same fellowship that he extends to all other believers.

As all commentators acknowledge, Paul does not explicitly go beyond this to ask for Onesimus to be manumitted, though this may be implied in verses 13-14, 21. Though Paul makes clear that Onesimus is precious (vv. 10, 12) and valuable to him (vv. 11, 13) we can only suppose that Philemon would have felt obliged, because of Paul's suggestion in verses 13-14, to send Onesimus back to Paul to work as Philemon's slave in Paul's service or to make him a freed person so that he could work alongside Paul.[48] If that is the implicit message, it stands in tension with the implied permanence of Onesimus's return in verses 15-16.

Paul's appeal is as compelling as it is vague. His persuasive artistry in Philemon combines rhetorical techniques, implied assertion of his authority and use of peer pressure suggested by the references to Philemon's Christian community. Paul directly addresses Philemon more than thirty times in this short letter, giving the impression that this is a personal appeal. But this letter is not merely private, for it is bracketed at the beginning and end by references to his coworkers and the church in his house (vv. 2-3, 22-25); the "grace and peace" formulae anticipate that the letter will be read when they are gathered for worship (vv. 3, 25).[49] Philemon's honor is on the line because his reaction to the letter would be scrutinized by his community. As Bartchy says, "His house-church was watching, and Paul hoped to be there soon to see for himself."[50]

This communal aspect in Paul's thought is not distinct from his understanding of life "in Christ" (vv. 8, 16, 20, 23).[51] Paul's appeal to Philemon is in the context of this shared life, as verse 6 suggests: as Philemon acts among the community so he acts toward Christ. Furthermore, since Paul in 1 Corinthians 12 teaches that the "body is one" (v. 12), Philemon's actions toward Onesimus "in Christ" are in effect actions toward Paul (v. 17). By identifying the community to which Philemon is accountable, Paul increases the likelihood that Philemon will obey (v. 21). Without resorting to a direct command, Paul makes a reference to compliance, a component that deserves further comment.

Against the backdrop of Philemon's watching community, Paul develops a distinction between commanding and appealing, a feature that is not peculiar to Philemon among Paul's letters.[52] He exploits his right "in Christ" to command (v. 8) only in order to contrast it with his loving appeal (vv. 9-10); thus he credits Philemon with the sense to freely do what is good and right (v. 14). Norman Petersen has demonstrated Paul's changing tone with the following table, where the second half of the letter (B1 and A1) mirrors the first half (A and B):[53]

A	B	B1	A1
command (8)	appeal (9-10)	consent (14)	obey (21)

It may be the case that Paul's open abandonment of a strong line of argument is itself a rhetorical technique wherein a point is made by denying that one is making a point at all *(antiphrasis)*.[54] However, because the request Paul makes of Philemon is "so oblique, so faltering," and because this is an uncommon feature of appeals in Greek letters, some further explanation for Paul's hesitation must be sought.[55] John Knox explains Paul's ambivalence in light of the weighty request, since Knox believes that Paul explicitly appeals for Onesimus to be returned to assist Paul in his missionary work: "I appeal for Onesimus."[56] However, the appeal is most naturally rendered "I appeal on behalf of,"[57] and Knox's view is somewhat undermined by verses 15-16.

John M. G. Barclay explains Paul's ambivalent appeal as an indication that Paul did not know what to recommend. Barclay suggests (1) that Paul was aware of the social difficulties of suggesting that a slave be freed and (2) that he pondered the irreconcilable nature of being truly "brothers" while remaining master and slave.[58] Against the first part of Barclay's argument, neither Greek nor Roman slavery was usually a permanent state, and owners could release bond servants for various reasons.[59] Many slaves may have had reason to expect emancipation by their thirtieth birthday and so Philemon's consideration may have been *when* and not *if* he would release Onesimus.

Against the second part of Barclay's argument, the incomprehensibility to us of how Philemon could remain both Onesimus's master and a brother would not necessarily have produced the same conflict of conscience for Philemon or Paul (though this may be the noblest implication of Gal 3:27-28). Patron-client relationships were a part of the fabric of society, paradoxically embracing the unstable combination of mutual solidarity and inequality of power—the very tension that is incomprehensible to us.[60] On our end of the interpretive bridge we are tempted to conclude, "It is logically and socially impossible to relate to one and the same person as both one's inferior and as one's equal."[61] This simply does not hold true for Paul's side of the interpretive bridge (compare 1 Cor 7:21-22; Eph 6:5-9; Col 4:1).[62] "Common sense" interpretations need to yield to realities of the cultural divide between Paul and us.

How then do we understand the ambivalence of the request Paul puts to Philemon, since he repeatedly appeals to Philemon's volition so he may freely choose the right thing (vv. 8-9, 14, 17, 20), all the while allowing the undercurrent of his authority to flow freely (vv. 21-22)? The answer may lie in Paul's leadership strategy of using his own personal example as a model for his converts. Paul's ambivalence itself may exemplify the attitude he wants Philemon to adopt in his reshaped relationship with his slave. As Paul refuses to assert the authority that he clearly possesses, Philemon is coached in the responsibilities of his newly reformed relationship with Onesimus. Paul wants to gain Philemon's consent so that he will freely do what is good, not by compulsion (v. 14). By this example the seed is sown for a new phase of the master's relationship with his slave. Paul does not compel Philemon to act, thus patterning for him a new style of interaction with his slave-become-brother, Onesimus.

Paul further models, consciously or unconsciously, how to be gracious and generous (v. 18). Though Onesimus's absence and wrongdoing caused Philemon a financial loss, Philemon may well have been able to cover this amount from his holdings of Onesimus's personal funds.[63] By offering to pay this amount Paul sets the tone for Philemon's future dealings with Onesimus. Generosity and liberality are highlighted as the marks of a Christian relationship of power (apostle with his convert), suggesting the liberality a master should display toward his slave.

Paul also portrays himself as an example of love (v. 9), a model Philemon has already followed (vv. 5, 7). Paul's display of compassion for Onesimus (v. 12) and his affirmation of Philemon's mercy toward other Christians (v. 7) are masterfully brought together in the identification of this same compassion as the appropriate behavior toward Onesimus "in Christ" (v. 22). There can be no doubt that Paul's love for Onesimus as "a beloved brother" (v. 16) is intended as an example for Philemon's relationship with his slave.[64]

Mary Ann Getty further suggests that the mention of Timothy may also serve as a model for the Christian master: "Paul wishes to give to Philemon an example of his own team ministry, with Timothy whom he joins to himself not as apostles possessing authority, but as servants. Paul is thus portrayed as one who lives and acts out [of] a communal context just as he exhorts Philemon to do."[65] At first this observation does not seem specific to Philemon, since Paul often makes references to his coworkers in his letters. However, there is a strong partnership theme in Philemon that gives support to Getty's observation. As N. T. Wright argues, Philemon is an outworking of the nature of "mutual participation" or "interchange" in Christ expressed in the idea of *koinōnia* (vv. 6, 17).[66] Implicitly, then, Paul presents his relationships with Timothy, Philemon and seven others in order to emphasize the community relationships to which Onesimus has gained entry by his conversion (vv. 1-2, 23-24).

Thus, Paul presents himself as an example of one who renounces his authority and is full of generosity, love and compassion for other members of the community of believers, in order that Philemon will emulate his example in his relationship with Onesimus (v. 21).[67] In Philemon, Paul exhibits self-restraint regarding his authority by explicitly refusing to command as he appeals to Philemon to freely forgive his grievance against Onesimus. This display of Paul's self-limitation of authority is combined with an example of love and generosity to model for Philemon how to treat his slave-who-has-become-a-brother.

Though Philemon has the legal right to be harsh with Onesimus, Paul asks him to grant Onesimus the same loving and generous treatment that he would extend to this elder missionary. That is because Onesimus has become a member of the Christian family as a beloved brother and a sharer in the missionary partnership. The community serves as a witness to Philemon's honor in carrying out the request of Paul, the elder who is in chains because of his gospel service. Paul's status as an elder and as Christ's metaphorical prisoner affirms Paul's authority in the community in the strongest terms, and his repeated emphasis on his imprisonment creates an emotional receptivity to his appeal (a rhetorical *captatio benevolentiae*). Whether or not Philemon would have or should have taken the letter as a suggestion that he manumit Onesimus cannot be ascertained, but it may be implied by verse 21: "I am confident of your obedience to the things I write, knowing that you will do more than the things I have asked" (my translation).

Thus, in Philemon we find a clear case of Paul's siding with a slave, appealing for his better treatment and his master's self-restraint, and it may well be that Philemon interpreted this letter as a call to manumit Onesimus, as the later Colossians 4:9 may indicate happened. Paul did not stand against the might of Rome by opposing all slavery everywhere, but he did stand with the slave Onesimus in his hour of need. This established a trend that was later developed in the early church.

Viewing Paul's Treatment of Slavery Through First-Century Glasses

The liberating tendency in Paul's letters was clearly perceived by the earliest Christians. For example, in his letter from Rome to Corinth, Clement writes about Christians who purchased ("ransomed") others from legal slavery at great sacrifice:[68] "We know that many among us have had themselves imprisoned, that they might ransom others. Many have sold themselves into slavery, and with the price received for themselves have fed others" (1 Clement 55:2). Writing from prison just after the turn of the first century, Ignatius, bishop of Antioch, wrote to Polycarp, bishop of Smyrna, about a problem current in their churches:

> Do not treat slaves, whether male or female, contemptuously, but neither let them become conceited; instead, let them serve all the more faithfully to the glory of God, that they may obtain from God a better freedom. They should not have a strong desire to be set free at the church's expense, lest they be found to be slaves of lust.[69]

Reading behind these remarks, it is clear that the Christian church in Smyrna was taking offerings to ransom slaves, and apparently Ignatius feared that slaves would start demanding it. The Shepherd of Hermas, from the same period, urges that Christians "ransom God's slaves from distress."[70] Obviously, another reason Christianity was attractive to slaves was that it offered them real help and not just contentment in the midst of their predicament.

Modern readers sometimes suppose that the opposite was true, but early Christianity was popular with slaves, as well as with women. Ted Turner, owner of CNN, has jabbed, "Christianity is a religion for losers." That is exactly how the slaves and women in Paul's day saw it. Even though proponents of slavery in the last century claimed Paul as their ally, he was, in fact, viewed in the first century as the troubadour of slaves. The problem with Paul is often a problem of perspective.

6

The Hebrew of Hebrews & Anti-Semitism

---

*O*ne-half of the Jews born in the last eight hundred years were murdered. One-third of the Jews who have lived in the last fifty years have been killed because they had Jewish parents.[1] Too often at the heart of these atrocities we find a mixture of religious and ethnic bigotry of Christians against Jews. I wince at the thought, but the problem of Christian anti-Semitism has been thought to have its roots in the teaching of the apostle Paul. If that is true, the problem of Paul takes on an immense and reprehensible moral dimension.

Is Paul partly responsible for the deaths and suffering of so many of his fellow Hebrews? It is true that just as Paul's texts were misused to uphold the cruelties of nineteenth-century slavery, so his comments were even more abused to fuel the fires of Auschwitz, attaching its own burden of disgrace to this Jewish apostle. But does this use of Paul's text find support in the text itself? Is it a legitimate interpretation of Paul?

Paul makes many strongly negative statements about "the Jews," and they have been echoed in the history of anti-Semitism, particularly in Hitler's Germany. Ever since Nazi Germany's genocide of the Jewish people, readers of the Bible have been jarred by racist-sounding comments when the phrase "the Jews" is used as a shorthand expression for "the bad guys"—those who are to accept all the blame for the crucifixion of Jesus or the difficulties of the early church. One such remark outside Paul's letters is "No one was brave enough to talk about Jesus openly, because they were afraid of the Jews" (Jn 7:13, my translation). Such a comment in the hands of the Nazis could easily be twisted to support a hatred of the Jewish people and to manipulate the masses to condone or overlook violence and injustice to their Jewish neighbors. The anti-Semitism of twentieth-century Germany has jaded our reaction to such phrases.

The purpose of this chapter is to explore four related questions: (1) Can Paul, a self-confessed "Hebrew born of Hebrews" (Phil 3:5; compare Rom 11:1), be fairly charged with anti-Semitism? (2) Do Paul's statements about the Jews support the anti-Semites who have often appealed to these passages? (3) Did Paul oppose Judaism, or did he see himself as a "good Jew"? (4) What do we make of Paul's abiding passion for Israel in Romans 9—11?

Distinguishing the Terms

There is a large body of recent literature on the question of the origins of anti-Semitism in the New Testament.[2] Throughout the literature, however, is a general lack of distinction between the terms *anti-Semitism, anti-Jewish, anti-Judaism* and *anti-Judaizing*. It is clear enough that Paul argues with other Jews in terms that shock our ears, but the key question for an enlightened interpretation is, What is the context of these remarks? There are three distinct ways that Paul's comments about Jews may be construed: as anti-Judaizing, as anti-Judaism or as anti-Jewish.

Anti-Judaizing is used to describe Paul's quarrel with Judaizers—Jewish *Christians* who thought that Gentile Christians should adopt a more Jewish lifestyle. When Paul argues with the Judaizers, it is purely anachronistic to equate Paul's ancient rhetoric against them with hatred of the Jewish people generally. Paul uses "Judaizer" in his letter to the Galatians to describe Jewish Christians who had strong convictions that Gentile Christians should be circumcised, follow Jewish dietary restrictions and observe the Jewish calendar (compare Gal 2:14). He sharply disagrees with their conception of the Christian life.

Anti-Judaism is used to mark theological disagreement with Judaism as a religion, often adopting a sharp, polemical tone. Paul's argument with the Judaizers, for example, is quite different from anti-Judaism, since his debate with Judaizers was both intra-Jewish and intra-Christian.

Anti-Jewish refers to hatred of the Jewish people that is embodied in discrimination, bigotry, abuse and, too often, physical violence. A synonym for anti-Jewish is anti-Semitism, the most common designation for prejudice against Jews as Jews, even though it is a misnomer. Since the nineteenth century, *anti-Semitism* has been used to signify *racial* hatred toward Jews, but this is not quite accurate. *Semite* includes a larger group than the Jewish people, incorporating also Arabs. Furthermore, Jewish people are not always Semitic—many Jews in Europe and the United States have blond hair and blue eyes, and Ethiopian Jews are black in racial background.[3] But because of the common use of the term *anti-Semitism* to refer to bigotry against Jews, it is used in this chapter to designate ethnic-religious social prejudice and persecution that are more accurately labeled *anti-Jewish*. Anti-Judaizing, anti-Judaism and anti-Jewish are terms that need to be kept distinct from each other.

Anti-Jewish	Hatred of the Jewish people that is embodied in a variety of forms, such as discrimination, bigotry, abuse and physical violence
Anti-Semitism	Used as a synonym for anti-Jewish, though technically it is a misnomer
Anti-Judaism	Theological disagreement with Judaism, often polemical in tone
Judaizers	Christian Jews who had strong convictions that Gentile Christians should be circumcised, follow Jewish dietary restrictions and observe the Jewish calendar

Was Paul Anti-Semitic?

Paul was not anti-Semitic. This is an anachronistic reading of the text. His comments about Jews are those of intra-Jewish polemics rather than anti-Jewish rhetoric.[4] Polemics were an expected element of effective ancient argumentation. Rather than reflecting Paul's bigotry against fellow Jews, Paul's attacking remarks indicate that he was an ancient communicator who was comfortable with the conventions of his culture. Several features found in his letters should lead us to reject the charge that Paul was anti-Semitic.

First, Paul was proud of his Jewish background.[5] To the Romans he identifies himself in clearly Jewish terms: "I myself am an Israelite, a descendant of Abraham, a member of the tribe of Benjamin" (Rom 11:1). To the Philippians he claims his heritage: "circumcised on the eighth day, a member of the people of Israel, of the tribe of Benjamin, a Hebrew born of Hebrews; as to the law, a Pharisee; as to zeal, a persecutor of the church; as to righteousness under the law, blameless" (Phil 3:5-6; compare Acts 22:3). Paul goes on in Philippians 3 to claim that he has found Christ to be more important than all the proud qualities of his Jewish identity. That does not make him anti-Semitic; rather, it serves to illustrate how important Christ had become for him. Although he had the very best Jewish credentials, his belief that Jesus Christ was the Jewish Messiah had taken on preeminence in his life. Even Paul's understanding of Jesus centers on the Jewishness of his Lord, whom he identifies as a descendant of the great Hebrew king David (Rom 1:3). Paul presents his Lord and his self-understanding in very Jewish terms.

A second reason we should reject the notion that Paul is anti-Semitic is that Paul explicitly counts Jews as equals with Gentiles. In fact, Paul's gospel is first for the Jews, but it extends also to the Gentiles: "I am not ashamed of the gospel; it is the power of God for salvation to everyone who has faith, to the Jew first and also to the Greek" (Rom 1:16). Throughout his letters, Paul takes pains to communicate that these two groups are equally plagued by sin and equally redeemed by God through Christ:

> There will be anguish and distress for everyone who does evil, the Jew first and also the Greek, but glory and honor and peace for everyone who does good, the Jew first and also the Greek. (Rom 2:9-10)

What then? Are we [Jews] any better off? No, not at all; for we have already charged that all, both Jews and Greeks, are under the power of sin. (Rom 3:9)

There is no distinction between Jew and Greek; the same Lord is Lord of all and is generous to all who call on him. (Rom 10:12)

Give no offense to Jews or to Greeks or to the church of God. (1 Cor 10:32)

Paul casts an egalitarian vision. His egalitarianism is even more important when we remember that Jews and Gentiles often were bitterly antagonistic toward each other, and Jewish response to Christians ranged from cold to cruel (see Gal 1:13-24).[6] Jews often despised Gentiles as "sinners" and "dogs," and Hellenists and Romans despised Jews as antisocial because of their unwillingness to participate in public life, largely due to Jewish unwillingness to fulfill the Greco-Roman social demand to offer libations to other gods and to eat idol meat in societal gatherings. Opposite to the charge of anti-Semitism, one of Paul's main concerns is to combat *Jewish* bigotry toward Gentiles. This is clearly the weight of Romans 3:29: "Is God the God of Jews only? Is he not the God of Gentiles also? Yes, of Gentiles also."

Furthermore, Paul uses typical Jewish, anti-Gentile rhetoric to side with Peter, only to immediately condemn the very attitude he adopts: "We ourselves are Jews by birth and not Gentile sinners" (Gal 2:15). Here, as in all Paul's letters, his confrontation with Jews and Jewish Christians is driven by his positive stance toward Gentiles and their culture.[7] For everyone's sake, Paul preaches the gospel of Christ, which builds a bridge of reconciliation over the Jewish-Gentile divide:

In the one Spirit we were all baptized into one body—Jews or Greeks, slaves or free—and we were all made to drink of one Spirit. (1 Cor 12:13)

There is no longer Jew or Greek, there is no longer slave or free, there is no longer male and female; for all of you are one in Christ Jesus. (Gal 3:28)

In that renewal there is no longer Greek and Jew, circumcised and uncircumcised, barbarian, Scythian, slave and free; but Christ is all and in all! (Col 3:11)

These texts emphasize the equality of Greeks and Jews, rendering unbelievable the thought that Paul was anti-Semitic or anti-Jewish. The evidence demands quite the opposite conclusion.

Use of "the Jews" in Paul's Letters

The problem of Paul and anti-Semitism may arise for modern readers, however, if we sample other sound bites, especially those containing the phrase "the Jews," from Paul's letters and weave them into an unfavorable portrait. But in each case, a fuller examination of the context of each passage shows no trace of anti-Semitism.

2 Corinthians 11:24. Here is one example of a supposed anti-Semitic text in Paul: "Five times I have received from the Jews the forty lashes minus one." At first glance, this looks like classic anti-Semitism, or, in Paul's case, what is sometimes called Jewish anti-Semitism. This bit of text, lifted from its context, seems like adding another log to the fire that fuels negative sentiment against Jews among his Corinthian readers. The context, which is all-important in responsible historical interpretation, dispels this mistaken notion, for Paul immediately goes on to say,

Three times I was beaten with rods. Once I received a stoning. Three times I was shipwrecked; for a night and a day I was adrift at sea; on frequent journeys, in danger from rivers, danger from bandits, danger from my own people, danger from Gentiles, danger in the city, danger in the wilderness, danger at sea, danger from false brothers and sisters. (vv. 25-26)

In this context Paul's statement about "the Jews" is not anti-Semitic; rather, it is a factual recounting of his many afflictions and opponents. He weaves them all together into a "hardship catalog," an ancient rhetorical device intended to increase the acceptance of one's advice, to endear one's readers to oneself and to demonstrate one's superiority, steadfastness and serenity amid struggle (compare 1 Cor 4:9-13; 2 Cor 4:7-12; 6:4-10).[8] A concise statement is found in Epictetus: "The difficult circumstances are those that show what men really are."[9] "The Jews" in 2 Corinthians 11:24 does not stand for all Jews everywhere, but for the five particular groups that whipped Paul. To confirm that this is not anti-Semitic, we should note that he also catalogs the danger he experienced from Gentiles and from other supposed Christians!

Philippians 3:2-4. Philippians 3 has often been taken as an anti-Semitic reference, but the question is far more complicated than it first appears in a clipping of the offending verses:

Beware of the dogs, beware of the evil workers, beware of those who mutilate the flesh! For it is we who are the circumcision, who worship in the Spirit of God and boast in Christ Jesus and have no confidence in the flesh—even though I, too, have reason for confidence in the flesh. If anyone else has reason to be confident in the flesh, I have more. (vv. 2-4)

Our first inquiry into Philippians 3 should be to determine the makeup of the opposition that Paul refers to here. It is probably mistaken to think that he is fighting against Jews as Jews. Paul does not argue against every Jew who believes in circumcision but against Christian Judaizers who exerted pressure to be circumcised and obey the Torah.[10] They "mutilate the flesh" (v. 2), a caustic description of the circumcision in which they "boast" (v. 3). Against them Paul asserts, "We . . . are the circumcision" who truly worship God (v. 3). Paul's Jewish self-presentation in verses 4-6 is contrasted with the Judaizers' emphasis on circumcision and the importance of "righteousness . . . from the law," a point made explicit when Paul repudiates his past (vv. 7-9).

Here is the crux of the matter: These verses cannot be used as evidence that Paul was anti-Semitic because it cannot be determined whether or not the Judaizers were Jewish or Gentile. It is true that "dogs" (v. 2) is a common Jewish pejorative for Gentiles, and this may be Paul's ironic use of a slur turned back on his fellow Jews.[11] Alternatively, it may be that the Judaizers Paul attacks with this phrase were Gentiles who pretended they knew better than he the requirements of the law for non-Jewish Christians. "Dogs" would then be Paul's *Jewish* Christian one-upmanship over Gentiles who promote circumcision, "the disdain of a real Jew for the Jewish fantasies of Gentile propagandists."[12] A third possibility is that "dogs" is being used as a general slur for one's enemies, whoever they may be (see Ps 22:16, 20; Is 56:10-11; 1 Enoch 89:41-50). The Philippians would know if these Judaizers were Gentile or Jewish, but we may never know for sure and are wrong to assume that the comments at the beginning of Philippians 3 are anti-Semitic.

Furthermore, it is most likely that these Judaizers were presenting themselves as Christians. There is no explicit indicator of this, just as there is in the case for some of Paul's opponents where he was imprisoned (Phil 1:15-18), but it is unlikely that Paul would need to warn the Philippians so sharply if these opponents did not have access to the Christian community (Phil 3:1-2).[13] Their Christian identity is further indicated by the parallel between the "deceitful workers" of 2 Corinthians 11:13, who clearly claim to be Christians, and the "evil workers" of Philippians 3:2. Paul's weeping for these antagonists (v. 18) does not, however, contribute to our identification of them, since he may be displaying a passion for either wayward fellow missionaries or for his fellow unconverted Jews (compare Rom 9:2).[14]

Philippians 3:19 is ambiguous and cannot be used to clarify the portrait of the opponents at Philippi. The phrase at issue is "their God is the belly; and their glory is in their shame." For some interpreters, this is simply a further indication of the Jewish nature of the opposition, referring to their scruples about keeping food laws, as commentators in the ancient church took this phrase.[15] A recent buffering of this interpretation is provided by Christopher Mearns, who argues that "belly" and "shame" are being used, as they sometimes are in the Greek Old Testament, as euphemisms for the male organ, further sarcastic references to circumcision (parallel to the biting use of "mutilation" in v. 2).[16] For other interpreters "belly" and "shame" are indicators that a Gentile libertine opposition is present,[17] either in their willingness to eat idol meat (compare 1 Cor 6:13; 8:1—11:1)[18] or of immorality in the more general sense of gluttony and sexual freedom.[19] Thus, it is possible to take the evidence of Philippians 3:19 as a reference to either Jews or Gentiles.

The evidence of Philippians 3 is that Paul's opponents were Judaizers and that, whatever their ethnicity, they were probably Christians. Philippians 3 is certainly not anti-Semitic and should not be understood as a swipe against Judaism. In Philippians 3 Paul wrangles with Christian Judaizers over the question of how much of the Jewish law Gentile followers of Christ should take on board. In Philippians 3, as in 2 Corinthians 11, Paul's comments are not anti-Jewish but are directed against Christian Judaizers.

1 Thessalonians 2:14-16. This is another problematic text, so troublesome that many interpreters feel that it could not have been written by Paul.[20] Since there is no manuscript evidence that this passage is an interpolation (a later insertion by a scribe or editor), another explanation must be sought for the harshness of these verses toward Jewish, non-Christian agents:[21]

> For you, brothers and sisters, became imitators of the churches of God in Christ Jesus that are in Judéa, for you suffered the same things from your own compatriots as they did from the Jews, who killed both the Lord Jesus and the prophets, and drove us out; they displease God and oppose everyone by hindering us from speaking to the Gentiles so that they may be saved. Thus they have constantly been filling up the measure of their sins; but God's wrath has overtaken them at last. (1 Thess 2:14-16)

This passage is polemical and highly emotional, but before we conclude that we find here a "smoking gun" in Paul's hand, we must consider two things.

First, Paul makes an analogy between the suffering of his Gentile converts in Thessalonica and that of the Jewish Christians in Judea. His purpose is to demonstrate that suffering should not be a reason for discouragement or disbelief, since it was the experience of the prophets, Jesus and the Judean Christians—in short, all who follow God's will. The Jews are not being vilified any more than the Gentiles who trouble the Thessalonian readers.

The emphasis in the letter is on how the Thessalonians' experience mirrors that of Paul and the Lord, as already announced in the opening verses: "You became imitators of us and the Lord, receiving the word among great affliction and with joy from the Holy Spirit" (1 Thess 1:6, my translation). Although it is true that the claim "the Jews killed the Lord Jesus" became the rallying cry of later Christian anti-Semitism, this is proof-texting, that is, lifting and misusing this line from Paul's first letter to the Thessalonians. In its original context, Paul identifies the crucifixion of Jesus with his readers' encounter of persecution to encourage them to be heartened by the similarity of their experience with their Lord's.

A second consideration we must keep firmly in mind is the earlier Israelite prophetic corrections of Israel and the use of polemic in the rhetorical education of Paul's day. Paul knew and stood in the tradition of the prophetic reform of Israel. Donald Hagner speaks for many scholars:

> Since Paul stands in the critical tradition of the prophets and Jewish apoc-
> alyptic, it makes no more sense to call him anti-Semitic in this passage than
> it does to call the prophets anti-Semitic. There is no racial hatred here. The
> language, harsh as it is, is spoken by a Jew to Jews and reflects the po-
> lemical idiom of an in-house debate.[22]

We must correct this slightly because 1 Thessalonians 2:14-16 is probably
addressed mostly to Gentiles in Thessalonica. Still Hagner rightly identifies
that this passage sounds more like the correctives of Paul's Old Testament
precursors than the ravings of twentieth-century Nazis.[23] For example, Elijah
uses the same kind of language about his fellow Jews: "The Israelites have
forsaken your covenant, thrown down your altars, and killed your prophets
with the sword. I alone am left, and they are seeking my life, to take it away"
(1 Kings 19:10, 14). It is probable that Paul derives his language from this
strain of polemic in his Jewish heritage, since he cites this very text in Romans
11:3.

The sweeping nature of the condemnation of Jews who reject the Messiah
Jesus—"they displease God and oppose everyone" (1 Thess 2:15)—reflects the
way argument and disagreement were conducted in Paul's day. As Luke Timothy Johnson correctly notes, "The way the New Testament talks about the
Jews is just about the way all opponents talked about each other back then."[24]
Paul is evenhanded in his use of this technique, applying it to Gentiles (Gal
2:15), Christian Judaizers (Gal 5:12) and Cretans (Tit 1:12).[25] Thus, Paul's
comments are at once those of intra-Jewish polemic and typical ancient rhetoric.

Do Paul's Statements Support Anti-Semitism?

So far I have given four reasons why charging Paul with anti-Semitism is
unjustified. First, he was proud of and heralded his Jewish background. Second, in several places he explicitly trumpets the equality of Jews and Gentiles,
and there is no place where he denigrates Jews as Jews. Third, many of Paul's
harsh comments are not directed first against fellow Jews but against fellow
Christians who taught that Paul was wrong to neglect circumcision, food laws

and the like. These Judaizers may have been Jewish, or they may have been Gentile converts to Judaism. Finally, sound bites of the phrase *the Jews,* in context, do not support the charge of anti-Semitism but place Paul's language firmly within the tradition of the prophetic reform of Judaism and the accepted ancient practice of polemics.

Paul was not anti-Semitic. The question remains, however, Does Paul set a trajectory in his letters that later flowered into full-blown anti-Semitism? This too we should answer negatively. If we went text by text through Paul's letters, we would conclude in each case that Paul's comments do not support anti-Semitism in any way, shape or form. The problem remains, however, that a pervasive connection exists between twenty centuries of Christian anti-Judaism and the evil anti-Semitic "final solution of the Jewish problem" in Germany between 1933 and 1945. To illustrate this, Sidney G. Hall III lists several examples of Nazi legislation paralleled in church law throughout the Middle Ages:[26]

☐ The law for the Protection of German Blood and Honor (1935) paralleled the Synod of Elvira (C.E. 306), which prohibited intermarriage and sexual intercourse between Christians and Jews.

☐ Jews were barred from train dining cars in 1939. The Synod of Elvira (306) forbade Jews' and Christians' eating together.

☐ The law for the reestablishment of the Professional Civil Service (1933) matched the Synod of Clement (535), which disallowed Jews to hold public office.

☐ A decree of 1938 allowed authorities to bar Jews from the streets on given days (such as Nazi holidays). The Third Synod of Orleans (538) inhibited Jews from showing themselves in the streets during Passion Week.

☐ The book burning in Nazi Germany paralleled the burning of the Talmud and other books during the Synod of Toledo (681).

☐ The 1940 *Sozialausgleichsabgabe* (Social Equalization Levy) enforced a Jewish income tax equal to the party contribution levied on Nazis. The Synod of Gerona (1078) forced Jews to equal Christian contributions to the church.

☐ Jews were forced to wear Star of David badges in 1941. The fourth Lateran Council of 1215 mandated the marking of Jewish clothes with a badge.

☐ Synagogues were destroyed in the entire Reich (1938). In 1222 the Council of Oxford banned the construction of new synagogues.

☐ Compulsory ghettos for Jews were ordered by Heydrich in 1939, echoing the compulsory ghettos legislated by the Synod of Breslau (1279).

☐ A 1939 decree mandated the sale of Jewish real estate. The Synod of Ofen (1279) forbade Christians to sell or rent real estate to Jews.

☐ Nazis passed a law against "Overcrowding of German Schools and Universities" in 1933, matching the Council of Basel (1434), which prevented Jews from obtaining academic degrees.

The list is sickening, repulsive and shameful. It does not matter that the parallels do not establish a necessary historical link between church canon law and Hitler's legislation that would satisfy a historian's canons of causation. The long trend in the Christian tradition to work out religious anti-Judaism in social anti-Jewish laws flowered in Hitler's Germany. This bleak thread of religious history and the ascendancy of the political madman converged. Hitler created a killing machine out of the latent religious and ethnic hatred of Jews found throughout Europe in his day. (And the anti-Semitism in European and American hate groups today is eerie and revolting.)

We have already noticed that Paul himself emphasizes an egalitarian view of Jews and Gentiles, unlike these two repugnant trails of historical tears (1 Cor 12:13; Gal 3:28; Col 3:11). How then can Paul be accused of supporting anti-Semitism? The charge is founded, plain and simple, on the age-old principle of guilt-by-association. It is unfair and often unfounded, but we sometimes operate on the principle that a friend of the enemy is also an enemy: if Paul's letters are used by anti-Semites, then he must be one too. The misuse of Paul's texts by anti-Semites and the importance of Paul for the anti-Jewish German reformer Martin Luther, have unfortunately and unfairly tainted the apostle's reputation.

Martin Luther (1483—1546), over the course of his life, gave evidence of a remarkable shift of opinion about the Jewish people. The earlier Luther wrote a pro-Jewish pamphlet entitled *Jesus Christ Was Born a Jew* (1523) to encourage Christians to treat Jews with respect and love. He argues against the anti-Semitic attitudes of leaders of his church, countering that Jews, like other people, can come to Christ; furthermore Jews were to be respected as Jews because Jesus was Jewish.

Nineteen years later, however, Luther showed a dramatic shift in his thinking when he penned *Against the Jews and Their Lies*. We hear a grim foreboding of what was to come:

What then shall we Christians do with this damned, rejected race of Jews? Since they live among us and we know about their lying and blasphemy and cursing, we cannot tolerate them if we do not wish to share in their lies, cursing, and blasphemy. . . .

First, their synagogues . . . should be set on fire. . . .

Secondly, their homes should likewise be broken down and destroyed. . . .

Thirdly, they should be deprived of their prayer books and Talmuds. . . .

Fourthly, their rabbis must be forbidden under threat of death to teach any more.

Fifthly, passport and traveling privileges should be absolutely forbidden to the Jews. . . .

Sixthly, they ought to be stopped from usury. All their cash and valuables of silver and gold ought to be taken from them.

Seventhly, let the young and strong Jews and Jewesses . . . earn their bread by the sweat of their noses as is enjoined upon Adam's children. . . .

To sum up, dear princes and nobles who have Jews in your domains, if this advice of mine does not suit you, then find a better one so that you may all be free of this insufferable devilish burden—the Jews.[27]

As a result, the next year (1543) Jews were expelled from Saxony. Luther became more deluded, preaching a sermon a few days before his death that all Jews should be driven from Germany. The result was the "age of the ghetto," as it was later called, during which the so-called Christian nations isolated and persecuted Jews for more than two hundred years. This is unmistakably the result of Luther's direct influence on religious and political powers after the Reformation. The Reformation historian Hans Hillerbrand cautions us, however, not to draw a direct a line from Luther's sixteenth-century anti-Semitism to twentieth-century Nazi Germany, for Hitler was influenced more by the seedbeds of anti-Semitism in Catholic Austria than those of Lutheran Scandinavia and Germany. When the complex historical picture is all accounted for, Hillerbrand argues, Luther played a minor role in later Nazi anti-Semitism.[28] Nevertheless, Luther became anti-Jewish in his own day, and his guilt is often extended to Paul because of the central place of Paul's quarrel with the Jewish law in Luther's theology.

Luther's interpretation of Paul was authoritative and highly influential until very recently. Only in the last two decades have critical scholars successfully challenged Luther's interpretation of Paul, particularly its anti-Jewish bent. In other words, it is not Paul *himself* who is the problem but the *misunderstanding* of Paul that has dominated New Testament interpretation for more than four hundred years. Luther's view that Judaism was a religion of works righteousness and moral straining after perfection has now been debunked.[29] The Judaism of Paul's day cannot be reduced to mere moral striving; furthermore, Paul's debates about the law are formed not against the backdrop of Judaism but as a defense of his advocacy of his gospel for the Gentiles.[30]

When Paul's statements have been used to support anti-Semitism, they have been misused. What we find in Paul are Christian in-house, intra-Jewish polemical statements. We should reject Nazi-like interpretations of these passages, and we also should reject using the pattern of ancient rhetoric that Paul employed. His ancient practice of communicating about fellow Jews is not a model for Christian relationships with Jewish believers. We live after the Holocaust, and "speaking the truth in love" (Eph 4:15) requires that we hear the clamor of Auschwitz echoing in our ears every time we say the words *Jews* and *Jewish*. This is not "political correctness" or hypersensitivity but common human decency. Christians who read such texts today must hear the pain of a whole people when such words are read and be quick to note that the comments in the Bible are mainly against other Christians (Judaizers) or corrective of Judaism by fellow Jewish adherents who saw themselves as reformers (see the next section). These comments in the New Testament are phrased in a way that a post-Holocaust Christian should never imitate.[31]

The apostle Paul himself sets the standard for Christian-Jewish relationships when he gives a clear directive on cultural and religious sensitivity. In

1 Corinthians 9:19-23, he outlines his own missionary principles, which he summarizes as "Never do anything that might hurt others—Jews, Greeks, or God's church—just as I, also, try to please everybody in every way. I am not trying to do what is good for me but what is good for most people so they can be saved" (1 Cor 10:32-33, my translation). If Paul occasionally takes the low road by echoing the harsh, caustic and exaggerated polemics of the prophets, here he points to the high road of considerate regard for others, regardless of their ethnic background.

Was Paul Anti-Judaism?

Paul was not anti-Semitic, and his letters undercut anti-Semites who would appeal to Paul. We must, however, come to some kind of understanding of what it was about Paul that evoked continual and violent opposition from his own countrymen. Obviously, many of them did not think he was simply a "good Jew." Therefore, several questions need answering: What is the nature of Paul's quarrel with Judaism? Did Paul see his Christianity as a reform movement from within Judaism, or did he view his new life in Christ as disjunct from his Hebrew heritage? What did Jewish believers find so distasteful in Paul's message?

How we answer these questions often depends on which passage in Paul's letters we are reading at the time. Differing pastoral situations evoked differing responses and emphases from Paul. We should also expect Paul's view to expand and develop over the fifteen or so years that he corresponded on the subject. A credible answer must take seriously two components of Paul's letters that are often difficult to hold together. First, a credible answer must recognize the continuity of Paul's teaching, reasoning and morals with those he acquired from Judaism, and it must account for his argument in Romans 9—11 for the continuity of the gospel of Christ with the promises and law of Israel. Second, a credible answer must account for the anti-Judaism elements in Paul's letters, such as his sharp rejection of circumcision, his liberal attitude toward idol meat and his downgrading of the importance of Moses. In other words, Paul's teaching demonstrates both a strong continuity and a marked discontinuity with Judaism, and our understanding of Paul's relationship with

Judaism must reflect these enigmatic features.

In the last twenty years, much scholarly attention has been paid to the Palestinian Judaism that Paul would have known and to the nature of Paul's relationship with Judaism, issuing in what has been dubbed "the new perspective on Paul." Although a new consensus has not been achieved, two points are widely asserted about what Paul opposed and how he understood himself as a Jew.

Paul's quarrel with Judaism. The "new perspective" is that Paul's main fight in his letters is not as a Christian against the "works righteousness of Judaism," as has been widely thought as a result of Luther's legacy in Pauline scholarship.[32] Scholars now realize that Palestinian Judaism cannot be fairly characterized as a religion of "works righteousness," since the emphasis in the documentary evidence falls upon fulfilling the law as a result of God's covenant with his people, not in order to gain God's acceptance. The so-called new perspective asserts that Paul reshapes the role of the law, not to attack a supposed works righteousness of Judaism but to allow for Gentiles to fully belong to the covenant people of God by their faith in Jesus Christ without adopting the practices of Jewish circumcision, diet and calendar observance.

Paul primarily addresses the questions that arise from the Jewish-Gentile Christian tension in his churches: How can Gentiles be included by faith in Christ without accepting all of the Jewish law, particularly circumcision and dietary observance? What is the place of the law in God's plan for the salvation of the world? The answers Paul gives are not always easy to understand or reconcile with each other, but Paul goes out of his way to claim that he upholds the Jewish law (Rom 3:31; 7:7).[33]

Paul's Jewish self-understanding. The new perspective on Paul is that he did not see himself as "anti-Judaism" but regarded his critique of Judaism from within the fold. He viewed Christianity as the fulfillment of Judaism. What Paul and the other New Testament writers "opposed in their polemicizing was in their eyes not truly Judaism but a truncated version of it, which tragically rejected its Messiah and which thus remained incomplete."[34] From Paul's point of view, he was not an outsider looking in at an alien faith; he was an insider looking out, standing within the tradition of prophets like Jeremiah who were "loyal opposition," fierce critics from within the community of Judaism.[35]

Before illustrating some elements of Paul's letters that are pro-Judaism, a note of caution must be sounded against misunderstanding the previous paragraph. Like beauty, "truncated Judaism" is in the eye of the beholder. Paul could just as easily be charged with abbreviating the religion of his ancestors, since he was the one who clipped circumcision from the program (Gal 5:2-6), soft-pedaled the issue of idol meat (Rom 14—15; 1 Cor 8—10) and downgraded the place of Moses and the law (2 Cor 3:6-18). Paul's deprecating references to Moses tend toward anti-Judaism, for Moses was the most important figure in the Jewish religion. Such slights on Moses and the law understandably provoked Jewish opposition, and that opposition sometimes issued in violence against Paul (2 Cor 11:23-25; Gal 5:11).

This makes evident that other Jews did not see Paul as he saw himself. Even Peter and other Jewish Christians vacillated concerning Paul's liberal stance (Gal 2). Circumcision, idol meat, table fellowship and the law were not small matters in the ethos of Israel, and it is difficult to overstate the problem that Paul's lax attitude on these matters presented for other Jews, both non-Christian and Christian Jews alike. After all, the Scriptures are clear on the "everlasting" nature of the covenant marked by circumcision:

> God said to Abraham, "As for you, you shall keep my covenant, you and your offspring after you throughout their generations. This is my covenant, which you shall keep, between me and you and your offspring after you: *Every male among you shall be circumcised.* You shall circumcise the flesh of your foreskins, and *it shall be a sign of the covenant between me and you.* Throughout your generations every male among you shall be circumcised when he is eight days old, *including the slave born in your house and the one bought with your money from any foreigner who is not of your offspring.* Both the slave born in your house and the one bought with your money must be circumcised. So shall my covenant be in your flesh an everlasting covenant. *Any uncircumcised male who is not circumcised in the flesh of his foreskin shall be cut off from his people; he has broken my covenant.*" (Gen 17:9-14, emphasis mine)

The words "I, Paul, am telling you that if you let yourselves be circumcised, Christ will be of no benefit to you" (Gal 5:2) are not easily reconcilable with the *everlasting* covenant given to Abraham. Christians are naive to underplay how hard these words of Paul hit the ears of other Jews. Indeed, Paul himself persecuted Christians before he turned to Jesus as the Messiah, *because he perceived Christianity as a threat to Judaism* (Gal 1:13-24). We must acknowledge that Paul's teaching, as much as he thought it to be a true fulfillment of the essence of Judaism, understandably provoked Jewish opposition. With that caveat, we can now look at four examples of Paul's positive stance toward Judaism.

1. Paul goes to the synagogue to spread his message about Christ (for example, Acts 13:5), and he submits to the discipline of the synagogue as one who belongs to the Jewish community. In his confrontation with the Jewish Christians in 2 Corinthians 11, Paul emphasizes both his stellar Jewish credentials (v. 22) and his greater willingness to toil and suffer on God's behalf (vv. 23-33). Several times he refers to how he received the discipline of the synagogue: "five times I received from the Jews the forty lashes minus one. . . . Once I received a stoning" (vv. 24-25). Paul continued to go to the synagogue, and he submitted to its forms of punishment again and again. That is not the behavior of a person who flatly rejected Judaism.

2. Further evidence for Paul's continuity with Judaism is his extensive use of the Jewish Scriptures. It would be difficult to imagine what would be left of Paul's letters if we attempted to clip out all references to the story of Israel. The stories about Adam and Eve and the world gone wrong, the Israelite bondage in Egypt for four hundred years and the deliverance led by Moses, and the giving of the law at Mount Sinai are essential for a full understanding of Paul's letters. To know Paul is to know Abraham, Sarah, Jacob, Moses, David, Isaiah and Jeremiah. The story of Israel is Paul's story too. His letters are the latest report on that larger, unfolding drama of God's relationship with his people. This essentially Jewish and profoundly foundational place of the Old Testament stories in the fabric of Paul's letters can be easily detected by English readers.[36]

The reader of Paul's letters in Greek is aware that Paul's use of many terms is highly dependent on the Greek translation of the Hebrew Scriptures called the Septuagint (abbreviated LXX). Where Paul does not cite from the LXX, he often and regularly alludes to it.[37] For example, in Romans 9—11 alone there are more than one hundred citations and allusions. Even in a letter with no explicit citation of the LXX, such as Philippians, the dependence is apparent. In Philippians 4:18 Paul praises the Philippians for their financial support in LXX ceremonial terms: "I am fully satisfied, now that I have received from Epaphroditus the gifts you sent, *a fragrant offering, a sacrifice acceptable and pleasing to God"* (compare Ex 29:18; Ezek 20:41). It should not surprise us that Paul's harshest criticism of unbelieving Jews (Rom 11:8-10) is a citation from the Old Testament![38] The examples could be multiplied many times over. To read Paul's letters is to read an author fully immersed in and dependent on the language of the Old Testament and the story of Israel.[39]

3. A third reason we cannot merely class Paul's teaching as anti-Judaism is because of how he made space in his mainly Gentile churches for principally Jewish religious scruples. For example, Paul's church in Corinth was mostly Gentile in makeup, but in 1 Corinthians 5—11 we witness Paul's struggle to inculcate his essentially Jewish understanding of right and wrong into a predominantly Gentile community. Paul's stance toward sexual immorality (1 Cor 5—7), lawsuits (1 Cor 6:1-9), idol meat (1 Cor 8—10) and women's place in the assembly (1 Cor 11:2-16) are distinctly Christian in outlook but imprinted with a Jewish framework and rationale. It is worth considering briefly his treatment of idol meat in 1 Corinthians, since it arises again as an issue in his letter to the church in Rome (Rom 14—15).

The law that Moses brought down from Sinai clearly made the rejection of idols a central sign of one's commitment to Yahweh, the God who had brought the Israelites out of Egypt (Ex 20:3-5). The Corinthians argued, and at first Paul apparently grants their point, that since there are no other gods but the one holy God, idols are nothing and meat sacrificed to them is not spiritually harmful (1 Cor 8). If we stopped there, Paul's apparent agreement minimizes a point that the Old Testament is unequivocal upon. But that is to read a section of Paul's letter without letting the flow and impact of the larger argument have its sway.

Already in 1 Corinthians 8 Paul prepares the way for his later argument by emphasizing their common ground of Jewish belief in only one God (vv. 4-6), and by 1 Corinthians 9—10 it is apparent that Paul has many firm things to say about how the Corinthian Christians are to face the issue of idol meat at their local market and at public meals.[40] Paul begins his approach in 1 Corinthians 8 by identifying the common ground he shares with them, and most scholars think that Paul quotes from their earlier letter to him (see 1 Cor 1:11; 5:1; 7:1). This is Paul's rhetorical and missionary strategy: he begins with common ground, builds a bridge and crosses over the religious and cultural divide for the sake of communicating the gospel (as he explains in 1 Cor 9:19-23; compare Acts 17:16-34). In 1 Corinthians 8 he gives them, initially, the sense that he agrees with their point. If he is quoting from their letter in verses 4-6, it is evident that they have already appropriated Jewish monotheism from Paul, even though they have not adopted the corresponding Jewish revulsion to meat sacrificed to idols.

The non-Jewish reader may not immediately feel the full force of what a Jewish reader cannot ignore: in 1 Corinthians 8 Paul may *sound* Jewish in his affirmation of monotheism, but he seems to waffle when he merely asks the Corinthians to deny themselves idol meat for the sake of another's weaker conscience.[41] Why does Paul not appeal to Moses' commands against idols if he has a Jewish conception of life in a Gentile city? This immediately cuts to the complexity of the question of Paul's attitude toward the law. The answer must reflect Paul's highly complex approach to a touchy and profound question for his mission as a Jew among Gentiles. At one and the same time he upholds the law, using it as a ground of ethical advice, but he also modifies its force and shapes its place in relation to those who have been "baptized into Christ." In fact, it is Paul's attitude toward the law that proves to be the major cause of opposition from within the Christian church, among other Jewish Christians.[42]

It is misguided, however, to form an opinion on 1 Corinthians 8 alone, when Paul deals with the matter through chapter 10. This additional context must be weighed before a conclusion is drawn about Paul's stance toward idol meat in Corinth. First Corinthians 8 calls for consideration of another's "weaker" conscience, but 1 Corinthians 9 adds three more weighty restrictions that increase the sense that Paul is against their eating idol meat: the authoritative personal example of the apostle Paul (compare 1 Cor 4:16; 11:1); the overriding concern for not inhibiting the spread of the gospel of Christ (1 Cor 9:12, 19-23); the emotional appeal to emulate the self-denial of an athlete's discipline (1 Cor 9:24-27).

To English readers, the full relation of 1 Corinthians 9:24-27 to the overall flow of Paul's argument may not be immediately apparent. To an ancient reader attuned to such rhetorical tricks-of-the-trade, however, the stirring image and the passionate appeal are an effective summary of the argument to this point and prepare the way for the more strict and austere words in the chapter that follows.[43] The athletic imagery of 1 Corinthians 9:24-27 would not be lost on the proud citizens of the host city of the Isthmian and Nemean games (which granted Corinth status akin to a modern city that hosts the Olympics). Paul baits his readers by beginning chapter 8 with an apparent casual concession, but by the end of chapter 9 Paul has increased the stakes and turned down the screws. His use of personal example, his appeal that they not limit the gospel work by their behavior and his appeal to athletic self-sacrifice, taken together with his already-mentioned concern for the "weak" of the community, leave his readers with the impression that he is not in favor of their open stance toward idol meat. He ends chapter 9 by urging them to be as stern with themselves as a runner or boxer in training, and he progresses to further restrictions in 1 Corinthians 10.

When we read on into 1 Corinthians 10, we find exactly what we expect if Paul's Jewish understanding were still influencing his moral reasoning. He proceeds to appeal to the conditions of the covenant given to Moses at Sinai and reiterates the Old Testament prohibition against idolatry twice (vv. 7, 12). Furthermore, he turns against the Corinthians and denies their casual attitude reflected in 1 Corinthians 8:4-6. Instead, Paul's Jewishness comes clearly to the foreground as he associates eating meat offered to idols with idolatry itself (1 Cor 10:14-22). He is a "liberal" Jew in his interpretation of this, however, since he does not consider idol meat to be a problem if the Corinthians do not know that it was sacrificed to idols (vv. 25-31), and he weights Gentile cultural sensibilities as equally important as Jewish ones (1 Cor 9:21; 10:27-29, 32). These three chapters in the middle of 1 Corinthians, taken as one example, make clear that Paul has not simply rejected the scruples of Judaism but continues to grapple with Jewish concerns among his Gentile converts. (For a slightly different approach to idol meat, see Rom 14—15.)

4. A fourth piece of evidence that Paul is not merely anti-Judaism is his regard for the abiding importance of the holy city, Jerusalem. He mentions Jerusalem ten times in his letters, and the references indicate Jerusalem's importance for him as the center of the spread of Christianity to the known world: "From Jerusalem and as far around as Illyricum I have fully proclaimed the good news of Christ" (Rom 15:19).

"From Jerusalem and as far around as Illyricum" is a phrase that sweeps geographically from one end of his mission to the other, from Jerusalem in the East to the northernmost point of his journeys in Greece.[44] The multiple references to Jerusalem in Romans are not merely an indication that the church began in Jerusalem; they highlight the significance of Jerusalem in Paul's thinking (Rom 11:26-27; 15:16, 19, 31).[45]

For Paul, there is an enduring place for Jerusalem and the church centered there. This is partly due to the central leadership of Peter (Cephas) and James in the Jerusalem church: "Then after three years I did go up to Jerusalem to visit Cephas and stayed with him fifteen days. . . . Then after fourteen years I went up again to Jerusalem with Barnabas, taking Titus along with me" (Gal 1:18; 2:1).

But there is more to Jerusalem for Paul than this. He raises money from the Gentile churches for the church in Jerusalem, and their material gift to Jerusalem reflects the spiritual gift of salvation that has come from Jerusalem to them (Rom 15:27). The Gentiles' offerings for Jerusalem are unparalleled by a corresponding collection for any other church:

> At present, however, I am going to Jerusalem in a ministry to the saints; for Macedonia and Achaia have been pleased to share their resources with the poor among the saints at Jerusalem. . . . [Pray for me] that I may be rescued from the unbelievers in Judea, and that my ministry to Jerusalem may be acceptable to the saints. (Rom 15:25-26, 31; compare 1 Cor 16:3;

2 Cor 9:1, 12)

Paul's trip to Jerusalem is obviously of great importance to him, but he makes clear that it has a place in salvation history. It may well be that Paul conceives of the offering for Jerusalem as a way to "provoke" Israel to faith in Christ, since his work among the Gentiles includes an agenda among the Jewish people, to save them by provoking their "jealousy" (compare Rom 10:19; 11:11-14). By implication, his apostleship to the Gentiles is ultimately an apostleship to Israel. In Paul's view, the Gentile offering is evidence for the Jerusalem saints that the ancient promises of Scripture are being fulfilled in the mission among the Gentiles (Rom 15:7-12).[46]

Earlier in Romans 15, Paul has already drawn attention to the imagery of priestly service in the temple in Jerusalem. He uses imagery from the temple worship in Jerusalem to describe his appointment by God "to be a minister of Christ Jesus to the Gentiles in the priestly service of the gospel of God, so that the offering of the Gentiles may be acceptable, sanctified by the Holy Spirit" (v. 16). In the Septuagint, "minister" *(leitourgos)* refers to priestly service in the tabernacle and temple, and this is what Paul has in mind when he uses the other sacrificial terminology of "priestly service" *(hierourgeō),* "offering . . . acceptable" *(prosphora . . . euprosdektos)* and "sanctified" *(hēgiasmenē).*[47] It is fairly clear that Paul considers the collection for Jerusalem to be a priestly offering for which he has been appointed; it is his priestly "ministry" for the ones in Jerusalem (compare 2 Cor 9:12; Phil 2:17, 30).[48] To be sure, Paul reinterprets the significance of Jerusalem, since he considers the temple worship to be replaced by the adoration of his Lord Jesus Christ (for example, Gal 4:24-26). Even so, Jerusalem maintains a high place in Paul's Christian rethinking of the values of Judaism.

Other cases could be considered, but the point is adequately made that Paul demonstrates both continuity and discontinuity with Judaism.[49] He cannot merely be considered anti-Judaism, but neither can he simply be labeled pro-Judaism. From his own point of view, Paul is probably better understood as a pro-Gentile, Jewish Christian apostle than as an anti-Judaist.[50]

The central issue for Paul is who Jesus Christ is and what his cross has accomplished. These issues remain a sticking point for his—and orthodox

Christians'—relationship with Judaism and secular society. So he writes to the Corinthians, "For Jews demand signs and Greeks desire wisdom, but we proclaim Christ crucified, a stumbling block to Jews and foolishness to Gentiles, but to those who are the called, both Jews and Greeks, Christ the power of God and the wisdom of God" (1 Cor 1:22-24).

Christ is the central distinction between the new "third race" *(tertium genus)* of Christians and their Jewish and Gentile parents. Paul refers to two cultures with which he was personally very familiar, coming from Jewish roots yet traveling widely in the Greek-speaking world. From his familiarity with both cultures, he notes some main reasons ancient persons did not accept Christ: some wanted to see miracles as proof that the message was true; others thought this message about Christ's death and resurrection sounded foolish. Yet Paul is adamant that this crucified Christ is the heart of the message that the earliest Christians believed and taught (1 Cor 1:30).

In Galatians 3, we cannot miss Paul's belief that Christ has displaced the centrality of the law. Paul is completely dependent on the story of Israel as exemplified by Abraham, but the story has now added the Christian chapter:

> In Christ Jesus you are all children of God through faith. As many of you as were baptized into Christ have clothed yourselves with Christ. There is no longer Jew or Greek, there is no longer slave or free, there is no longer male and female; for all of you are one in Christ Jesus. And if you belong to Christ, then you are Abraham's offspring, heirs according to the promise. (vv. 26-29)

For Paul, to be a Christian is to stand in the line of tradition that reaches all the way back to this father of the Jewish people. Thus, Paul lays the groundwork for a downplaying of Jewish-Gentile divisions and heralds the creation of a third race made up of both Jews and Gentiles.

This is evident in Ephesians 2, which is written from a Jewish standpoint and is firmly grounded in the imagery of Judaism. Yet the understanding of these symbols from Judaism is totally restructured because of Paul's conviction of the centrality and significance of Jesus as the Christ, the Jewish Messiah:

> So then, remember that at one time you Gentiles by birth, called "the

uncircumcision" by those who are called "the circumcision"—a physical circumcision made in the flesh by human hands—remember that you were at that time without Christ, being aliens from the commonwealth of Israel, and strangers to the covenants of promise, having no hope and without God in the world. But now in Christ Jesus you who once were far off have been brought near by the blood of Christ. For he is our peace; in his flesh he has made both groups into one and has broken down the dividing wall, that is, the hostility between us. He has abolished the law with its commandments and ordinances, that he might create in himself one new humanity in place of the two, thus making peace, and might reconcile both groups to God in one body through the cross, thus putting to death that hostility through it. So he came and proclaimed peace to you who were far off and peace to those who were near; for through him both of us have access in one Spirit to the Father. So then you are no longer strangers and aliens, but you are citizens with the saints and also members of the household of God, built upon the foundation of the apostles and prophets, with Christ Jesus himself as the cornerstone. In him the whole structure is joined together and grows into a holy temple in the Lord; in whom you also are built together spiritually into a dwelling place for God. (Eph 2:11-22)

This is pro-Gentile, but it is written from a Jewish point of view, obvious in the references to circumcision, the temple, the prophets, "the commonwealth of Israel" and "the covenants of promise." This Jewish viewpoint has been revamped, however, by the reconciling significance of Christ's blood. Christ "has abolished the law with its commandments and ordinances," since through him Gentiles and Jews are reconciled into "one new humanity" and both "have access in one Spirit to the Father." The significance of the Jewish prophets is complemented by the appearance of the Christian apostles, and the centrality of the temple in Jerusalem is displaced by the universal presence of the spiritual temple of the Christian church.

If we can see in these passages a noble view of one united humanity, we must remember that this ideal is based on a conviction that Jesus is the Jewish Messiah and that the importance and purpose of Jewish law has been displaced by the new covenant, which is based on trust in the importance of the blood of Christ. Paul did not perceive these beliefs as anti-Judaism, but those who reject Jesus as the Messiah and retain the importance of the law as taught in the Hebrew Scriptures would find both of these assertions difficult to swallow. A parting of the ways was inevitable, and paradoxically as Christ reconciles Jews and Gentiles in the church, the Crucified One remains the source of division between the church and Judaism.[51] Paul's comment about his "earlier life in Judaism" (Gal 1:13-14) may merely imply that at that point he saw himself as a convert from one form of Judaism (Phariseeism) to another (Christianity).[52] It was only a matter of time, however, before the two roads diverged for good.

Paul's Abiding Passion for Israel

Paul is pro-Christ but not anti-Jewish. If Paul's preaching disposed Christians and Jews to a parting of the ways, he never abandoned his love and passion for his own people. Even though he rejects some key components of his "earlier life in Judaism" (Gal 1:13), he has not written off the Jewish people. This is seen most clearly in his extended treatment of the subject in Romans 9—11.

Paul takes his differences with other Jews very personally, and his compassion and grief are apparent in Romans 9—11. In these three chapters Paul develops his theological understanding of the place of both Israel and the Gentiles in the salvation plan of God. He defends God's faithfulness to his promises as he shows from the Old Testament why the promise extends also to the Gentiles (Rom 9:24; 11:13). They receive the blessings of God's promises by faith (Rom 9:30). Equality abounds in this aspect of Paul's theology, because salvation is by faith for everybody, Gentile and Jew alike (Rom 10:4, 9-13). Those who do not have faith in Christ are under judgment. Therefore, Israel's rejection of Christ is a very serious matter, and the potential rejection of Israel deeply disturbs Paul (Rom 9:2, 31; 10:2; 11:7-12, 14-23).[53]

Throughout these chapters Paul's personal feelings for his fellow Jews emerge. In Romans 9:2-5 he feels so strongly that he says he is willing to sacrifice himself so that other Israelites could come to his Christian faith:

I have great sorrow and unceasing anguish in my heart. For I could wish that I myself were accursed and cut off from Christ for the sake of my own people, my kindred according to the flesh. They are Israelites, and to them belong the adoption, the glory, the covenants, the giving of the law, the worship, and the promises; to them belong the patriarchs, and from them, according to the flesh, comes the Messiah, who is over all, God blessed forever. Amen.

He repeats this evangelistic passion at the beginning of the next chapter: "Brothers and sisters, my heart's desire and prayer to God for them is that they may be saved" (Rom 10:1). In Romans 11:1 he uses himself as a test-case for the assertion that God has not rejected his people. His argument runs, paraphrased, as a simple syllogism:

God has not rejected me.

I am an Israelite.

Therefore, God has not rejected Israel.

Naturally, Paul views this retrospectively from his Christian perspective.[54] He modifies this claim in what follows, asserting that the rejection of Israel is only partial (Rom 11:1-10), is only temporary (vv. 11-27) and there is a purpose in all this beyond human comprehension and wisdom (vv. 28-36).[55]

Paul's desire is for Israel to come to know Christ as he has. He holds out great hope for the salvation of Israel, "if they do not persist in unbelief" (Rom 11:23), that is, if they do not continue to reject Jesus as the Messiah.[56] If they do accept Jesus as the Messiah, they too "will be grafted in" (see vv. 23-29). Paul believes that Jews remain "beloved, for the sake of their ancestors" (v. 28). It would be difficult to find a more pro-Jewish statement, although it is set in the context of pro-Christian theology by this Jewish apostle of Christ.

Paul is not anti-Semitic; he is pro-Gentile. Paul is anything but anti-Jewish, though his ancient, intra-Jewish rhetoric has sometimes mistakenly been interpreted that way. Elements of his letters are critical of Judaism, but these must be balanced against the many ways Paul presents himself as "a good Jew." Paul demonstrates both continuity and discontinuity with his ancestral religion. The division comes because he believes that a crucial change has happened with the coming of Christ, the one whom he proclaimed throughout the Roman empire as the Jewish Messiah.

7

Paul's Problem Personality

*I*n the previous chapters we have pondered Paul's viewpoints and sayings that are often controversial in our day. When Paul's remarks are viewed in their ancient context first, he is much less controversial and we can better understand and appreciate his effectiveness as a missionary. This chapter deals with a different type of criticism about Paul: attacks on his personality and doubts about his behavior:

What sort of man was Paul?—Not by any means a saint. Goodness was far from being his most notable characteristic. He was proud, unbending, imperious; he was self-assertive and masterful; he used hard words; he believed that he was absolutely right; he stuck to his opinions; he quarreled with many people.[1]

This list of criticisms is long, but several of these charges can be defused: Paul himself claimed to be the chief of sinners (1 Tim 1:15); he candidly confessed to pride (Phil 3:3-11); he openly admitted that he did not always know the right course (1 Cor 7:12; Phil 1:22); he was often on the defensive against the attacks of others, making his quarrels unavoidable. Furthermore, Paul said that he was far from perfect: "Christ Jesus came into the world to save sinners—of whom I am the foremost" (1 Tim 1:15; compare Phil 3:12). This disclaimer should prepare us for what we find: Paul exhibits all the signs of the human condition—the faults and foibles to which we all are heirs.

Even so, some serious questions remain about how noble a character Paul really was. The question is not "Was Paul perfect?" for Paul himself has already given us a negative answer. What we should ask is this: Is Paul *worse* than average? Does his practice of setting himself as a model for others make his imperfections count that much more against him (for example, 1 Cor 4:16; 11:1; Phil 3:17; 4:9)? Does he miss the mark by a greater distance than a human leader should?

In this chapter three kinds of criticisms that have been leveled at Paul are examined and weighed: (1) his behavior is unloving; (2) his personality is unchristian; (3) he displays deep psychological flaws that drive his thinking, especially regarding his views on sex and women.

Paul's Bad Behavior

First, we should consider how Paul behaved. Of course, we have not witnessed his actions in person, so our best sources are his thirteen letters and the witness of the book of Acts.

We do not need to consider Paul's murderous mission against Christians (Acts 8:1; 9:1-2), since the whole point of this portrait is to demonstrate the dramatic change that happened to him when he met the risen Jesus on the road to Damascus (Acts 9:1-30). Paul himself confesses to this earlier life of persecuting Christians (Gal 1:13) and to the subsequent and amazing turn-around that happened when God "was pleased to reveal his Son to me" (Gal 1:15-16). This about-face was astounding enough for Luke to repeat three times (Acts 9, 22, 26), and Paul quotes others who observed his remarkable reformation: "The one who formerly was persecuting us is now proclaiming the faith he once tried to destroy" (Gal 1:23). For them, Paul tells us, his transformation could only be an act of God. His former life was reprehensible, but he admitted it, recanted of his past and acknowledged that God had been exceedingly merciful to him (1 Cor 15:9-10). There is no reason to dredge up this part of Paul's past and hold it against him.

Our question is, What explanation is there for Paul's cutting remarks, apparent inconsistency and use of shame to motivate his converts *after* he met Christ? Why does Paul not always appear to live up to his own standards, sometimes seemingly transgressing statements he has made in the same letter? (Compare, for example, Gal 5:12 and 6:1.)

Paul used cutting remarks and name-calling. Did Paul always "speak the truth in love" (Eph 4:15)? The apparent answer is no. In the heat of battle, and often motivated by deep concern for the spiritual well-being of his churches, Paul struck out with harsh, polemical remarks and called his opponents unkind names. This accusation is softened when we remember that this was how opponents generally addressed each other in antiquity, and Paul obviously took seriously the eternal risk that his converts were facing (compare Mt 18:6-7). Even so, could he not have rebuked his opponents in a more charitable manner, particularly since they considered themselves to be a part of the Christian family (compare Mt 18:15-17)? He himself said, "My friends, if anyone is detected in a transgression, you who have received the Spirit should restore such a one in a spirit of gentleness" (Gal 6:1). Does this counsel square with his own practice in the following remarks?

For such boasters are *false apostles, deceitful workers, disguising themselves* as apostles of Christ. And no wonder! Even Satan disguises himself as an angel of light. So it is not strange if *his ministers* also disguise themselves as ministers of righteousness. Their end will match their deeds. (2 Cor 11:13-15)[2]

But because of *false believers* secretly brought in, who slipped in to spy on the freedom we have in Christ Jesus, so that they might enslave us. (Gal 2:4)

You *foolish Galatians!* Who has bewitched you? (Gal 3:1)

I wish those who unsettle you would castrate themselves! (Gal 5:12)

Beware of the *dogs,* beware of the *evil workers,* beware of those who *mutilate* the flesh! (Phil 3:2)

It was one of them, their very own prophet, who said, "Cretans are always liars, vicious brutes, lazy gluttons." That testimony is true. For this reason rebuke them sharply, so that they may become sound in the faith. (Tit 1:12-13)

On the surface, then, it appears that Paul did not always "restore such a one in a spirit of gentleness." But there may be other factors for us to consider before we assume that he has violated his own counsel in each of these cases. For instance, in the example from Titus 1:12-13, Paul's concern is that the whole church will be undone by the false teaching on the isle of Crete. Paul believes that false teachers and individual transgressors need to be dealt with differently. False teachers who shake the church need to be rebuked sharply, whereas gentle correction is afforded individual transgressors (Gal 6:1).

Paul agrees with the exaggerated stereotype of a famous Cretan poet, Epimenides, whom Titus's companions on Crete would respect (although the letter is addressed to Titus, it is clearly written for hearing by the Christians on Crete). It may strike us that Paul has moved beyond the bounds of polite argument, but his citation of a *Cretan* authority to *Cretans* increases the effect of his corrective to these ancient readers. Here Paul utilizes the tools of ancient rhetoric to sway his readers in favor of conforming to Titus's leadership. On our end of the interpretive bridge it would be wrong for us to speak about people of other nationalities in this way, but the Christians on the island of Crete would have taken Paul's comments differently.

Words can be bad to some people but not to others. We attach feelings to words like *Satan* and *fool,* but often we are unaware that others do not have those same negative feelings about the exact same phrases. This can be illustrated from our own language in the slightly different cultures of America and Great Britain. I am an American writing this chapter in Yorkshire, a northern county of England. I learned growing up that telling someone to "shut up" is rude and a put-down. You can imagine my shock when I moved to Yorkshire some years later and found "Oh, shut up" to be a totally acceptable way of saying "Oh, don't be silly." On the other hand, many an American has said "bloody" in Britain, unaware that they have used the foulest swear word available on the other side of the Atlantic. Such connotations are difficult to explain because they are the result of complex social learning and reinforcement.

Once a British preacher was totally unaware of how easily his sermon on Ephesians 2 could be misunderstood when he delivered it on a preaching tour in America. In Britain, one sits on one's "bum," and, when the word *but* is heard, no one would ever think of one's posterior. Of course, *but* and *butt* sound exactly the same when spoken—only the context can determine which is meant. One Sunday morning this poor soul, victim of the great divide of ocean and language, announced that his message about God's exceptional love in Christ was entitled "But God" (Eph 2:4). He struggled through his four-point sermon to the growing confusion and giggles of his American audience. Every time he said *but* he meant *except,* but his listeners heard the word that he would have used for *bum.* His four points:

1. God has a but.

2. We all have buts too.

3. Some of our buts are bigger than others'.

4. The only problem with your but is that you are the only one who can't see it!

If the connotations of words are quite different in the same language in slightly different cultures, how much more is this true when we experience Paul's words and assume that they were as insulting in his day as they seem to us. We have to keep this in mind when Paul calls his opponents in Corinth servants of Satan and his followers in Galatia foolish. If these were said of us, we would feel heavily criticized and embarrassed. At one moment Jesus can call Peter "blessed" and "the rock" on whom he will build his church (Mt 16:17-18) and a few verses later label him "Satan" because Peter did not realize the importance of Jesus' coming crucifixion (Mt 16:23). Obviously, the label did not imply a permanently damned state as it might to us (compare 1 Cor 5:5).

Conversely, we might not get too excited if someone said "anathema" to us (NRSV, "accursed"), but, when Paul uses this Aramaic curse as a double warning in Galatians 1:8-9, he sounds the sharpest possible alarm available to him (compare 1 Cor 12:3). "Bad" words are culturally determined, and we must be careful not to read our connotations into Paul's rhetoric. His opponents found his letters "weighty and strong" (2 Cor 10:10), and this was partly due to his ability to utilize the accepted rhetorical conventions of his day. When we consider how we talk about others in our quite different culture, we need to find appropriate ways to live up to Paul's wise counsel: "My friends, if anyone is detected in a transgression, you who have received the Spirit should restore such a one in a spirit of gentleness" (Gal 6:1).

Paul was inconsistent and hypocritical. A different criticism of Paul's behavior arises from this previous discussion: Paul does not live up to his own espoused values and so is hypocritical. It may not appear that he always restored others in the spirit of gentleness that he urged on others. In one place he condemns "people pleasing" (Gal 1:10) and elsewhere he appears to promote it (1 Cor 9:19-23; 10:32-33; Rom 15:1-3). This, however, is merely an *apparent* inconsistency, since in 1 Corinthians and Romans Paul is discussing indifferent matters of conscience. If the communities in Corinth and Rome were to overlook others' concerns about idol meat, their casual approach could cause serious harm to the community. In these cases he calls for adapting to the needs of the community.

In Galatians 1:10 and 2:4-5, 11-14, on the other hand, Paul gives his personal example of how the Galatians should stand firm against the Judaizers. He goes on to demonstrate for them how he was not a people pleaser in Jerusalem (Gal 2:4-5), nor with Peter in Antioch (Gal 2:11-14). Paul gives in Galatians 1:10 a thematic statement that he develops in the letter, much like Romans develops the theme in Romans 1:16-17 and Philippians expounds Philippians 1:21-22: "Am I now seeking human approval, or God's approval? Or am I trying to please people? If I were still pleasing people, I would not be a servant of Christ" (Gal 1:10).

This statement should be read in light of the overall argument of the letter before it is compared with the texts in 1 Corinthians and Romans. The Galatians are to follow Paul's succinctly stated personal example in Galatians 1:10 (compare Gal 4:12), a literary technique he uses throughout his letters.[3] He models for his Galatian readers appropriate interaction with those who require circumcision. It is in relation to this specific group that they are not "people please." To give in to their demands would be to abandon the gospel of grace that he taught them (Gal 1:6-9; 5:1-2). This principle from Galatians 1:10 is quite different from regarding others' feelings on indifferent matters (Rom 15:1-3; 1 Cor 9:19-23; 10:32-33).

A case could be made that Paul is inconsistent in how he handles his financial support as a missionary. In Corinth and Thessalonica he made a big deal of his self-support as a tent-maker, and he reminds both churches of this when he writes to them later (1 Cor 9; 1 Thess 2:1-12; 2 Thess 3:6-13). A critic could point out the discrepancy between Paul's boast of financial independence from the Corinthians and his effusive thanks to the Philippians for their generous support (Phil 4:10-20). Is this inconsistency?

Paul's financial practice varies, but this is probably better labeled *adaptation* than *hypocrisy*. Paul's practice in Corinth and Thessalonica is not the standard for Christian missionaries, who expect financial support from their gospel labor. Paul argues for the right to missionary support in 1 Corinthians 9, only to emphasize that he has not claimed it. This self-denial is presented as a model for the Corinthians, who are then asked in turn to give up eating idol meat. We should not fault Paul for accepting his rightfully due missionary support from Philippi but, rather, should praise his admirable self-sacrifice in Thessalonica and Corinth. Also, we should not overlook that his material needs and ability to get employment would not be evenly spread wherever he went and that his situation had changed dramatically from his earlier letters (1 Thessalonians, 1 Corinthians) to the time some years later when he wrote to the Philippians from jail. In jail he needed and received financial support, but when he wrote to Corinth and Thessalonica he was a free man and able to support himself. Paul should not be charged with inconsistency on principles of financial support. Such a charge echoes modern scandals of television preachers whose lives are a far cry from this dedicated missionary who often barely lived at a subsistence level (see Phil 4:10-20).[4]

Paul used shame to motivate his converts. It is indisputable that Paul used shame as a way of motivating and shaping his churches in his absence. Stated so bluntly, on our side of the interpretive bridge this sounds appalling. Before we consider the use of shaming on Paul's cultural end of the bridge, here are a few examples of his use of this accepted practice in antiquity.

In his effort to raise money from Corinth for the church in Jerusalem, he uses shame as a fund-raising technique: "Otherwise, if some Macedonians come with me and find that you are not ready, we would be humiliated—to say nothing of you—in this undertaking" (2 Cor 9:4). To the "lazy" in Thessalonica, who would not work to earn their keep, Paul organizes the community to shame them back to work: "Take note of those who do not obey what we say in this letter; have nothing to do with them, so that they may be ashamed" (2 Thess 3:14).

Paul may implicitly use this same technique in Philemon by making multiple references to Philemon's watching community. If Philemon does not do what Paul asks, his honor may be turned to shame before all those who heard Paul's instructions to him. In 1 Corinthians 4:14 we are left wondering what Paul might have written to require this disclaimer: "I am not writing this to make you ashamed, but to admonish you as my beloved children." Why does Paul need to say this unless something he said could be misconstrued as a shaming remark?[5] It may be that the Corinthians would feel shame that Paul, their spiritual father, endured an inferior status and degrading treatment (1 Cor 4:6-13) while they, his children, enjoyed the very best. This is one source of shame that Aristotle identified: "It is also shameful not to have a share in the honorable things which all men, or all who resemble us, or the majority of them have a share in."[6]

Shame and honor were pivotal issues for the ancient world.[7] The shame-culture in earlier Greek times was concerned with public esteem and honor rather than the enjoyment of a quiet conscience. The classicist E. R. Dodds tells us, "The strongest moral force which Homeric man knows is not the fear of god, but respect for public opinion."[8] The shame-culture gradually became a guilt-culture, but the significance of honor and shame persisted in Paul's day. Furthermore, shaming was an accepted rhetorical weapon and an approved feature of public discourse.[9] On our end of the interpretive bridge, we find it repugnant to use shame as a fund-raising or disciplinary technique, but this would not have been the case in Paul's day (and perhaps in many of the shame-based cultures around the globe that still exist). We cannot fault Paul for living within the conventions and values of his quite different, ancient culture.

Paul's Arrogance and Egotism

We move from a consideration of how Paul behaved (what he did and said) to a consideration of his character (who he was). Many readers form the impression that Paul was an arrogant person, hardly a desirable personality characteristic for one who claimed to be Christ's ambassador and to speak for God: "We are ambassadors for Christ, since God is making his appeal through us; we entreat you on behalf of Christ, be reconciled to God" (2 Cor 5:20). And yet it is this very claim that some think is arrogant. What kind of humble person, they might ask, considers himself one of God's coworkers (1 Cor 3:9; 2 Cor 6:1)? Isn't it grandiose to claim that you have been set aside from birth for your task (Rom 1:1-2; Gal 1:1, 15)?

That may be how it seems to an unsympathetic critic, but Paul stands in the long line of Jewish prophets who felt destined to be God's mouthpieces. The critic who says there is no such thing as a humble person who claims to speak for God has already judged Paul and the prophets on this matter. In Paul's mind, however, his confidence did not come from himself (arrogance) but from God, who had given him his message and commission (1 Cor 9:17). He knew that this message sounded foolish, yet it had been entrusted to him (1 Cor 1:17—2:5). He felt compelled to speak on behalf of Christ, and a sense of dread trailed him if he did not: "If I proclaim the gospel, this gives me no ground for boasting, for an obligation is laid on me, and woe to me if I do not proclaim the gospel!" (1 Cor 9:16).

For those who can accept that God calls, gifts and sets apart individuals for special works, Paul had an admirable and enviable sense of purpose and destiny, a conviction that must have kept him going during many a dark night in prison, nursing his bruises and recovering from abuse. No one follows a trembling trumpet, and Paul exhibited the confidence found in so many effective leaders. He claimed that it was God-given confidence (1 Cor 1:30-31).

Two recent writers have thought that Paul displays egotism and a self-centered personality in other ways in his letters. Nicholas Taylor, for example, thinks that a careful reading of Galatians reveals that Paul portrays his apostleship as "egocentric and individualistic," and he conjectures that this results from Paul's sense of isolation after his Antioch conflict with Peter recounted in Galatians 2:11-14.[10] Taylor's psychological interpretation of Galatians requires that Paul "lost" this confrontation with Peter in Antioch, but I find this dubious. In the middle of a pitched battle to keep his converts in Galatia from "Judaizing," why would Paul mention a failed attempt at confronting Peter? Why would he raise counter-evidence against himself when he considers the issue so critical (Gal 1:6-9)?

A more critical question that Taylor's hypothesis cannot answer is, Where in the text do we find evidence that Paul "lost" this disagreement with Peter? It is much more straightforward to suppose that Paul recounts his confrontation with Peter to support his argument against the Judaizers in Galatia. The impression of Galatians 2:11-21 is that Paul presents this as evidence that he was right—and Peter and the Galatians know it. Furthermore, it seems that Paul presents his autobiographical remarks in Galatians 1—2 in order to underline the God-given nature of his message rather than to draw attention to himself for his own sake. This is clearly the sense of Galatians 1:1, 10-12. Galatians does not give us evidence that Paul was egotistical, and the interactions in Galatians 2 are anything but individualistic.

In an article provocatively entitled "Philippians: Paul's Most Egocentric Letter," Robert Fortna asserts that this letter shows that Paul was "primarily preoccupied with himself" and that "Philippians is surely Paul's most self-centered letter, the most subtly arrogant of all—before God and the world."[11] As one of Paul's most personal letters, Philippians employs *I, me,* and *my* more than fifty times,[12] which could give the impression of self-centeredness. But that overlooks two features of Philippians as a somewhat typical Greco-Roman letter: (1) characteristics of a letter of friendship, where personal information is essential; (2) the common practice of Hellenistic moralists and later rabbis to present themselves as models in their teaching. Fortna misinterprets the function of Paul's self-references, labeling them "self-absorbed" and "grandiose." Paul explicitly presents his own personal example and the pattern of others for emulation by his readers in good Greek style (compare

Phil 2:1-11; 3:17; 4:9).[13]

Contrary to Fortna's approach, we should give full weight to the Greco-Roman principle that a good letter should substitute for one's personal presence, a feature that Paul accomplishes quite nicely in Philippians. It is evident that the Philippians were very interested in—even financially committed to—the subject of the letter, having sent Epaphroditus to care for Paul and deliver their material support (compare Phil 2:17, 25, 30). It would have seemed strange to them—after sending money to Paul and expressing deep concern about his predicament (Phil 1:19)—if Paul wrote back to them in impersonal terms about the state of the missionary enterprise. Such an approach might sound less egotistical to a modern critic's ears, but it would have been bad manners from the Philippians' viewpoint. It is difficult to suppose that Paul should do anything else than discuss himself and present his own personal example in Philippians.

Paul was certainly confident and bold as a leader, and these characteristics may be kissing cousins of arrogance. My impression is that Paul had plenty of negative experiences, set-backs, opposition and failures to keep him humble and dependent on God's divine guidance and strength. This, at least, is what he says about himself throughout 2 Corinthians (and see Phil 2:18-26; 3:12-21). If Paul was a robust leader, this is a remarkable and necessary component of his missionary effectiveness, given the opposition he encountered. I find Paul not "arrogant" but incredibly buoyant, unashamedly hopeful and strong in trust for what God would do:

> We are afflicted in every way, but not crushed; perplexed, but not driven to despair; persecuted, but not forsaken; struck down, but not destroyed; always carrying in the body the death of Jesus, so that the life of Jesus may also be made visible in our bodies. For while we live, we are always being given up to death for Jesus' sake, so that the life of Jesus may be made visible in our mortal flesh. So death is at work in us, but life in you. But just as we have the same spirit of faith that is in accordance with scripture—"I believed, and so I spoke"—we also believe, and so we speak, because we know that the one who raised the Lord Jesus will raise us also with Jesus, and will bring us with you into his presence. (2 Cor 4:8-14)

Paul's Neurotic Notions

Someone has said that we are all neurotics, with occasional bouts of temporary sanity. Anyone with teenagers in their household will quickly confirm this overgeneralization. Paul, it should be thought, was also a normal neurotic. If he was "normal," his neuroses should not create a problem for us. The problem arises when certain views of his are identified as deriving from his neurotic personality and past traumas rather than from his understanding of Scripture and through a revelation of Christ, as he claims. After all, many people claim they speak for God when really they are projecting their own views, their own brokenness, their own psyches, on the rest of the world. Does Paul fit this category? Were his views about singleness, sex and marriage derived from his unhealthy psyche and from psychologically unresolved traumas in his past?

In our post-Freudian, pop-psychology-saturated society, it is common to hear glib explanations of why people act or think the way they do based on some past trauma or a breach in their relationship with their parents. As we might expect, there are no limits to imaginative explanations about why Paul viewed marriage, sex and singleness in the way he did. For example, early in the modern psychological age, Gerhard Delling conjectured that Paul came to his views on marriage and women because his mother died when he was young, depriving him of an appreciation of family life, since he had to be raised by men.[14] Such an explanation is tempting because of its simplicity, but Delling's creativity is fanciful and unfounded. There is simply no historical support for this psychological analysis. How do we know Paul's mother died when he was young? How do we know Paul was raised by men? We have no evidence for this whatsoever. (Fathers might further object to the sexist suggestion that they cannot create a sense of family life.)

Further conjectures about Paul's past and psychological formation of his views on marriage, while serving to discredit Paul, are speculative and unhelpful. Instead, we have seen that Paul's views on sex and marriage have a clear and explicit historical and theological explanation. From his Jewish background Paul knew the purpose of marriage as depicted in Genesis 2:22-24: that a man and a woman become "one flesh" (compare 1 Cor 6:15-16; Eph 5:31). Likewise, his cultural environment gave him every reason to suppose that the hierarchical relationships of husband and wife, child and parent, slave and master were the normal order of affairs. We need not seek psychological xplanations for Paul's views on matters that are clearly grounded in his religious and cultural heritage.

The same is true when we come to Paul's views on the single life. Unkind explanations suggest that Paul was hung up on sex, that he hated women, and this comes through in his loathing of marriage. This line of psychological conjecture, however, misinterprets Paul and overlooks the plausible reasons Paul gives for his views. Those who claim to understand the psychological motives of others must show significant reserve when applying their art to historical figures such as Paul. There are three main problems with psychological analyses of Paul as a historical personage: the problem of the nature of our sources, the problem of falsification of our hypotheses and the inherent problem of crosscultural psychological explanations.

The limitation of our sources. Our sources are textual and very scant. Paul wrote thirteen letters that are known to us (at most). Those letters are highly conventional in two ways. Their form is conventional; much of the letter—the greeting, the well-wishing, the body and closing—are prescribed for the writer. Paul's letters may tell us more about his good Greco-Roman manners than his psyche. Second, strategies of ancient rhetoric left their imprint on all aspects of communication, and Paul's letters are no exception. Many of the elements of Paul's letters that strike us as odd or negative may have had the reverse effect on his early readers. This is even the assessment of his opponents in Corinth, who concede, "His letters are weighty and strong" (2 Cor 10:10). In other words, we cannot simply suppose that the impression that Paul's letters make upon us is actual, relevant psychological information about him. This, it seems to me, is Fortna's mistake about Philippians and Taylor's mistake about Galatians. Rather, many elements of his letters were conscious or unconscious concessions to the rhetorical demands of his cultural setting. These layers of convention and rhetoric in Paul's letters do not allow us to reasonably suppose we possess an unfogged window to Paul's psychological makeup.

The problem of falsifying our hypotheses. A second and rather obvious observation is that any conjectures we make or hypotheses we form about Paul that are not supported by textual evidence are simply that—fanciful conjectures and illegitimate arguments from silence. If there is no way to falsify or verify one's hypothesis, is it a worthwhile hypothesis? Fiction and fantasy are entertaining, but we overstep when we present creative imaginings as historical explanations.[15]

A good example is our lack of knowledge of what Paul looked like. The earliest physical description of Paul comes from the end of the second century. It may preserve a historical memory when it mentions that Paul was bald, since early catacomb paintings depict Paul with little hair: "a man of small stature, with a bald head and crooked legs, in a good state of body, with eyebrows meeting and nose somewhat hooked, full of friendliness."[16] Our initial impression of this description is quite different from what the context reveals. We might suppose—wrongly, but predictably—that this is a pejorative depiction of Paul's physical appearance. This conclusion is exactly opposite of the truth.

The passage goes on in the next line to show the somewhat glorified portrait that is being painted: "Indeed at one moment he looked like a man, and at the next he seemed to have the appearance of an angel." Richard Bauckham says, "The modern impression that this is an unflattering description is mistaken. According to ancient ideas about physiognomy, the hooked nose, bowed legs and meeting eyebrows were regarded favorably, and shortness was not necessarily a disadvantage."[17]

Things are not always as they seem. Historical knowledge is based on texts, and those texts need to be interpreted in light of their cotexts and contexts before we race to historical judgments about the events or persons they depict. Since this is true with physical descriptions, our caution should be great when we attempt psychological profiles.

The questionable legitimacy of crosscultural, transhistorical psychological analysis. A third point, on which I have no expertise but only hunches, is that we are not guaranteed that psychological motivations and explanations are crossculturally transferable. For example, theories about the formation of gender roles and identity are highly debated within one culture—our own.[18]

Our gender explanations are not easily transferred across cultural groups in the twentieth century, let alone applying the tentative observations of our postmodern, twentieth-century, Western world to people of ancient societies. If we had adequate textual information to make an assessment (which I doubt), and if we adequately factored in and filtered out the conventional and culturally idiosyncratic forms of rhetoric in those texts (which often may be impossible), we still may not know enough to make an adequate psychological assessment of a person who lived and breathed two millennia ago. Consistently throughout this book I have countered and cautioned against anachronisms, and here I add the caution against cultural imperialism, presuming that our culturally conditioned, psychological explanations work for other cultures in other places and times.[19]

God's Treasures in Earthen Vessels

If we were talking about your pastor in this chapter, few people would counter that their spiritual leader has no human faults. (In my experience, most are eager to chime in with more!) When we go to church on Sunday, we value the message that is preached not because we think that our pastors are perfect but because they are credible witnesses to who Christ is and to what he has done for us on Good Friday, Easter Sunday and Pentecost. We do not fault Christian leaders for being imperfect, but we do expect them to stay free of flagrant faults. If they do or say things to lose their credibility, then their character becomes the main issue. We can no longer hear their witness to Christ when we no longer think they are credible witnesses.

All this, of course, applies to Paul too. If we begin to accept some or all of the charges that have been lodged against him—that he is anti-Semitic, racist, sexist, hypocritical, cutting, sarcastic, arrogant, egotistical, psychologically disturbed—then at some point these accusations make Paul a noncredible witness to Christ. But we have found these charges to be unfounded, overstated or more a result of our cultural differences than reflective of Paul's personality problems.

Paul was not a perfect person. He himself makes clear that he had clay feet and remains in the realm of the normal neurotic, a front-runner with me and you for the title of "foremost sinner." We do not need to pretend that his letters present a perfect person, since he reminds us, "Not that I have already obtained this or have already reached the goal; but I press on" (Phil 3:12).

In 2 Corinthians 10—13 Paul's opponents criticized him for not being perfect and tried to use this as a means to undermine the message by undermining the messenger. Their reasoning went something like this:

1. God uses perfect bearers for divine revelation.

2. Paul has obvious troubles, weaknesses, health problems, speech deficiencies and lacks the power of the Spirit.

3. Therefore, Paul is no real apostle and should be ignored.

Out of his conflict with these "false apostles" in Corinth (2 Cor 11:13), however, Paul gives us a different kind of divine calculus, one that values how God uses fallible human beings for his infallible purposes:

1. God has chosen to use faulty human beings to show that the power is from above and not of human origin.

2. Paul is a faulty human being.

3. Therefore, Paul's faults do not disqualify him as an apostle but qualify him for God's use and redemption.

Paul said this in so many words: "We have this treasure in clay jars, so that it may be made clear that this extraordinary power belongs to God and does not come from us" (2 Cor 4:7). The "treasure" is the divine gospel and the "clay jars" are the weak vessels God is pleased to use. (This, by the way, is why we can call a Sunday-morning sermon "God's word" even though we know the imperfections of the plain Jane or John who happens to be speaking.) Paul's assertion is that God works this way to keep us from thinking that somehow we possess, control or dispense God's liberating power. Later in 2 Corinthians, Paul passionately describes how he wanted God to remove his "thorn . . . in the flesh" (2 Cor 12:7-8), some kind of physical weakness that was discrediting Paul to the Corinthians:[20]

Three times I appealed to the Lord about this, that it would leave me, but he said to me, "My grace is sufficient for you, for power is made perfect in weakness." So, I will boast all the more gladly of my weaknesses, so that the power of Christ may dwell in me. Therefore I am content with weak-

nesses, insults, hardships, persecutions, and calamities for the sake of
Christ; for whenever I am weak, then I am strong. (2 Cor 12:8-10)

Paul's weaknesses qualify, rather than disqualify, him as God's messenger! It
is not Paul's perfection but his witness to Christ that reveals God's message,
a message that many people—then and now—find to be God's power and
strength for living in an often perplexing and difficult world filled with sinful,
imperfect and broken people, Christian and non-Christian alike.

8

Paul
on His
Best Day

---

*T*he purpose of this book has been to explore problems that Paul's letters present to a modern reader, to raise awareness of how our cultural context affects our interpretation of the Bible and to encourage a conversation with Paul and his interpreters. Perhaps Paul has always been followed by criticism. In his lifetime, he was dogged by various charges:

1. Some Corinthians, inspired by antagonists of Paul, thought that his suffering, physical weakness and speech deficiencies were evidence that he was no true apostle. This may have been true in Philippi also.

2. Many Jewish Christians could not accept his dismissal of the importance of circumcision and food laws. Even Peter had difficulty with this (Gal 2:11-14).

3. Others were violent against Paul because they disagreed with his views, because he was causing civic controversies or because his teaching threatened their livelihood (see Acts 16:16-24).[1]

As if this were not enough, the author of 2 Peter candidly tells us how difficult it was sometimes for early Christians to understand what Paul was saying: "Paul wrote to you according to the wisdom given him, speaking of this as he does in all his letters. There are some things in them hard to understand, which the ignorant and unstable twist to their own destruction, as they do the *other* scriptures" (2 Peter 3:15-16). In this simple statement, we have a very early witness to two features of Paul's letters: they were sometimes difficult to understand, and they were already regarded at this early stage as authoritative writings, implied by the phrase, "as they do the other scriptures."

It is this last feature that has been the source of the controversy surrounding Paul. If he had been considered a heretic and his writings neglected, we probably would not be bothered by the values in his letters that are very much like other writings of his day. It is when these letters, with all their cultural baggage, are elevated to the level of God's revelation that the difficulty arises. Nevertheless, we are able to cross over the cultural divide and retrieve the divine message, the treasure contained in cultural clay jars. This interpretive crossing requires careful attention and humble reflection and is aided by a conversation with many others who wrestle with the same texts and issues.

Paul, though sometimes puzzling, is not always a problem. Many people have found in Paul something revealing, liberating and Christ-centering. Martin Luther said of his own journey, "In the scholastics I lost Christ but found him again in Paul." Karl Barth, a major German theologian of the twentieth century, has said, "If we rightly understand ourselves, our problems are the problems of Paul; and if we be enlightened by the brightness of his answers, those answers must be ours."[2]

I have found this last statement to be true not because when I look into Paul's letters I identify with Paul (though that is sometimes true) but because again and again it is their Christ-centered nature that I find so revealing. Although we are sometimes puzzled by parts of Paul's letters, it is no mystery that his life and thought and ethical views flow from his understanding of life "in Christ." His descriptive statements about who Christ is and what Christ has done become the foundation for his instructions to his converts. His teaching is centered on Christ: "For we do not preach ourselves, but Jesus

Christ as Lord, and ourselves as your slaves on account of Jesus" (2 Cor 4:5, my translation).

In our day, social ethics play an important role in public discourse. Paul did not live in that kind of world. He was a missionary, not a senator of the Roman Republic. Few others in his day could comment on social policy, and disagreement with the emperor could be deadly. Paul was a practical missionary, who subordinated social ethics to his driving purpose to make the resurrected Christ known. This was his determining end and justifying means. He expected his churches to adopt his same missionary posture by doing whatever it took (within limits) to make the message of Christ known to Greeks, Romans and Jews. Thus, his missionary program included pragmatic, culture-specific instructions on how women should behave in church and how wives, husbands and slaves should behave in their homes. Many of these social injunctions were means to his missionary end, often questions of strategy and etiquette rather than principle.

If the missionary means Paul employed in his day are no longer appropriate to ours, we still must ponder his witness to the end goal of his effort: "I want to know Christ and the power of his resurrection" (Phil 3:10). It is, after all, his testimony to the risen Lord that so many have identified with through the centuries, securing for Paul a permanent place in the affections of believing Christians. Throughout the ages they have found in Paul's teaching a way to describe their own spiritual experience of life in Christ. As Paul Tillich, the twentieth-century theologian, has said, "To the [person] who longs for God and cannot find him; to the [person] who wants to be acknowledged by God and cannot even believe that he is; to the [person] who is striving for a new imperishable meaning of his life and cannot discover it—to this [person] Paul speaks."[3]

Though Paul remains trapped as a prisoner of history, a fate we all share, he communicates timeless and transcendent truth about the crucified and resurrected Jesus as God's plan for our redemption. The strength of Paul's teaching about Christ far outweighs the problems Paul's historical conditioning and human foibles may create for us. My heart's desire is that the conversation with Paul that has been engaged in these pages will always yield to the more important and timeless conversation with the One for whom Paul lived. Paul stands, arms linked with the other key leaders of the earliest church—fully admitting his deficiencies as a person—and proclaims:

For I handed on to you as of first importance what I in turn had received: that Christ died for our sins in accordance with the scriptures, and that he was buried, and that he was raised on the third day in accordance with the scriptures, and that he appeared to Cephas, then to the twelve. Then he appeared to more than five hundred brothers and sisters at one time, most of whom are still alive, though some have died. Then he appeared to James, then to all the apostles. Last of all, as to one untimely born, he appeared also to me. For I am the least of the apostles, unfit to be called an apostle, because I persecuted the church of God. But by the grace of God I am what I am, and his grace toward me has not been in vain. On the contrary, I worked harder than any of them—though it was not I, but the grace of God that is with me. Whether then it was I or they, so we proclaim and so you have come to believe. (1 Cor 15:3-11)

Notes

Chapter 1: The Problem with Paul

[1]Peter Cook and Dudley Moore, "Religions," in *Dud and Pete: The Dagenham Dialogues* (London: Methuen, 1971), pp. 138-39.

[2]J. Christiaan Beker, *Heirs of Paul* (Minneapolis: Augsburg/Fortress, 1991), pp. 100-101.

[3]S. Scott Bartchy, "Slavery (Greco-Roman)," in *Anchor Bible Dictionary*, ed. David N. Freedman (New York: Doubleday, 1992), 6:67.

[4]For a compendium of the difficult passages in Paul's letters, see Manfred T. Brauch, *Hard Sayings of Paul* (Downers Grove, Ill.: InterVarsity Press; 1989). For a moderate approach to many of these same issues, see Ernest Best, *Paul and His Converts* (Edinburgh: T & T Clark, 1988), and Robert Jewett, *Paul, the Apostle to America: Cultural Trends and Pauline Scholarship* (Louisville, Ky.: Westminster/John Knox, 1994). For an extreme and unsympathetic approach to Paul, see Graham Shaw, *The Cost of Authority: Manipulation and Freedom in the New Testament* (London: SCM Press, 1983).

[5]In scholarly circles this is disputed, and many suggest that Paul became a specific kind of *Jewish* missionary for the Messiah. For example, see James D. G. Dunn, *The Partings of the Ways Between Christianity and Judaism* (London: SCM Press, 1991).

[6]Cited in Malcolm Muggeridge and Alec Vidler, *Paul, Envoy Extraordinary* (London: Collins, 1972), p. 14.

[7]Stanley K. Stowers, *The Diatribe and Paul's Letter to the Romans,* Society of Biblical Literature Dissertation Series 57 (Chico, Calif.: Scholars, 1981).

[8]E. Earle Ellis, "Paul and His Co-workers," *New Testament Studies* 17 (1971): 437-52.

[9]For example, Romans 16:22. Compare 1 Corinthians 1:1 and 16:21; 1 Corinthians 4:17; Philippians 1:1; 1 Thessalonians 1:1-2; 2:18—3:6.

Chapter 2: The Male Chauvinist & the Modern Woman

[1]Many scholars think that 1 Timothy was not written by Paul, and the issues are summarized in Werner Georg Kümmel, *Introduction to the New Testament,* trans.

H. C. Kee, rev. ed. (Nashville: Abingdon, 1975), pp. 370-84. A recent defense of Paul's authorship is made by Luke Timothy Johnson (*The Writings of the New Testament: An Interpretation* [Philadelphia: Fortress, 1986], especially pp. 255-57) and by George W. Knight III (*The Pastoral Epistles: A Commentary on the Greek Text* [Grand Rapids, Mich.: Eerdmans, 1992], pp. 21-52). If 1 Timothy 2 was written by someone else, it still presents us with the same problem of interpretation because it is in the Christian canon. Regardless of authorship, I treat the issue here as "the problem of Paul."

[2]Gerda Lerner, *The Creation of Feminist Consciousness: From the Middle Ages to 1870* (New York: Oxford University Press, 1993), p. 17.

[3]Robin Scroggs has undertaken this same sort of project in "Paul: Chauvinist or Liberationist?" *The Christian Century* 89 (1972): 307-9; "Paul and the Eschatological Woman," *Journal of the American Academy of Religion* 40 (1972): 283-303; and "Paul and the Eschatological Woman: Revisited," *Journal of the American Academy of Religion* 42 (1974): 532-37. However, Scroggs is comfortable dismissing Ephesians and 1 Timothy as non-Pauline and appears to believe that this eliminates them from consideration in the problem of Paul. I am attempting to clarify a way of dealing with all such texts in the canon of Scripture, whether they were written by Paul or not.

[4]Jerome Murphy-O'Connor, *Paul on Preaching* (London: Sheed & Ward, 1964), pp. 59-60.

[5]Elisabeth Schüssler Fiorenza, "Missionaries, Apostles, Co-workers: Romans 16 and the Reconstruction of Women's Early Christian History," in *Feminist Theology: A Reader,* ed. Ann Loades (London: S.P.C.K., 1990), p. 61. The definitive study on Paul's use of envoys and letters as a substitute for his authoritative presence is Robert W. Funk, "The Apostolic *Parousia*: Form and Significance," in *Christian History and Interpretation: Studies Presented to John Knox,* ed. W. R. Farmer, C. F. D. Moule and R. R. Niebuhr (Cambridge: Cambridge University Press, 1967), pp. 249-68.

[6]Cited in Lerner, *Creation of Feminist Consciousness,* p. 71.

[7]See E. Earle Ellis, "Paul and His Co-workers," *New Testament Studies* 17 (1971): 437-52; Wolf-Henning Ollrog, *Paulus und seine Mitarbeiter: Untersuchungen zu Theorie und Praxis der paulinischen Mission* (Neukirchen-Vluyn, Germany: Neukirchener, 1979).

[8]Chrysostom *Epistle to the Romans* 31; cited in Florence M. Gillman, *Women Who Knew Paul* (Collegeville, Minn.: Michael Glazier, 1992), p. 67.

[9]See Gillman, *Women Who Knew Paul,* pp. 66-69, for an authoritative treatment.

[10]The word *apostle* tends to be used in the book of Acts to designate one of "the Twelve." This difference of usage reminds us that words take on certain connotations given them by their author's usage, and there is no reason for us to assume that Luke

and Paul should have the same "idiolect" (an individual's pattern of using words with a specific connotation).

[11]Cf. 1 Corinthians 15:10; 16:16; Galatians 4:11; Philippians 2:16; Colossians 1:29; 1 Thessalonians 5:12; 1 Timothy 4:10; 5:17; 2 Timothy 2:6.

[12]I owe this insight to a conversation with sociologist Don Liebert of Whitworth College.

[13]On the difficulties and the relationship of 11:5 and 14:33-36, see Ralph P. Martin, *The Spirit and the Congregation: Studies in 1 Corinthians 12—15* (Grand Rapids, Mich.: Eerdmans, 1984), pp. 83-88.

[14]So also Gordon Fee, *The First Epistle to the Corinthians,* New International Commentary on the New Testament (Grand Rapids, Mich.: Eerdmans, 1987), pp. 522-24.

[15]See Beverly Gaventa, "Apostles as Babes and Nurses in 1 Thessalonians 2:7," in *Faith and History: Essays in Honor of Paul W. Meyer,* ed. J. T. Carroll, C. H. Cosgrove and E. E. Johnson (Atlanta: Scholars, 1990), pp. 193-207.

[16]See Beverly Gaventa, "The Maternity of Paul: An Exegetical Study of Galatians 4.19," in *The Conversation Continues: Studies in Paul and John in Honor of J. Louis Martyn,* ed. R. T. Fortna and B. R. Gaventa (Nashville: Abingdon, 1990), pp. 189-201.

[17]Mary Stewart van Leeuwen, *Gender and Grace: Love, Work and Parenting in a Changing World* (Downers Grove, Ill.: InterVarsity Press, 1990), p. 36.

[18]Henry Chadwick, *The Early Church* (Baltimore: Penguin, 1967), pp. 58-59.

[19]Lerner, *Creation of Feminist Consciousness,* p. 140. The approach of Scroggs, cited above, seems to me to fall into the revisionist category.

[20]There is some question on the location of 1 Corinthians 14:34-35 (some manuscripts placing them after v. 40), but there is no question of their antiquity. G. W. Trompf ("On Attitudes Toward Women in Paul and Paulinist Literature: 1 Corinthians 11:3-16 and Its Context," *Catholic Biblical Quarterly* 42 [1980]: 196-215) wants to question Paul's authorship of 1 Corinthians 11:3-16, despite the absence of any ancient manuscript evidence. This approach strikes me as deliberately revising Paul's text because of preconceived notions of what he could or could not have said.

[21]G. B. Caird, "Paul and Women's Liberty," *Bulletin of the John Rylands Library* 54 (1972): 268-81.

[22]Fee, *First Epistle to the Corinthians,* p. 512.

[23]Catherine Clark Kroeger and Richard Clark Kroeger (*I Suffer Not a Woman: Rethinking 1 Timothy 2:11-15 in Light of Ancient Evidence* [Grand Rapids, Mich.: Baker Book House, 1992]) offer a reconstruction of the situation behind 1 Timothy 2:11-15 that limits its scope very specifically to the problems in Ephesus, namely that the passage called on the women of Ephesus to learn the truth and to refrain from teaching

Gnostic-like error. On this view we would expect 1 Timothy 1:20 to mention women rather than men (Hymenaeus and Alexander). Furthermore, we are left without an explanation for the entire letter's propensity to give instruction along gender lines, which leaves the impression that the instructions in 1 Timothy reflect a conception of different roles for men and women (see especially 2:15 and also 2:11, if interpreted more straightforwardly as in the traditional interpretation). The Kroegers offer many helpful insights and survey both the various approaches to this text and many relevant aspects of women in the Greco-Roman social world. I am left with the impression, however, that their view is a modified form of revisionism, weighted heavily on a reconstruction that changes the more obvious and straightforward sense of the text at hand. For a brief and more text-centered interpretation, see Colin Kruse, "Human Relationships in the Pauline Corpus," in *In the Fullness of Time,* ed. D. Peterson and J. Pryor (Homebush, Australia: Lancer, 1992), pp. 167-84.

²⁴Craig S. Keener, *Paul, Women and Wives: Marriage and Women's Ministry in the Letters of Paul* (Peabody, Mass.: Hendrickson, 1992).

Chapter 3: Paul on the *Oprah Winfrey Show*

¹Leon F. Bouvier and Carol J. De Vita, "The Baby Boom—Entering Midlife," *Population Bulletin* 46, no. 3 (Washington, D.C.: Population Reference Bureau, 1991).

²Not everyone wants to adhere even to these rules. NAMBLA (North American Man-Boy Love Association) is content with rule one (two people can do as they please as long as no one is harmed) but rejects rule two (children must be protected from adult sexual advances). Others want to debate what an "adult" is. The British Parliament recently lowered the age of sexual consent from twenty-one to eighteen, meaning that it is no longer a crime for an adult to have sex with an eighteen-year-old. As before, those under eighteen years old can freely have consensual sex with others under eighteen without committing a crime.

³This last category is found in his condemnation of homosexual practices in Romans 1, employing the argument that it is "contrary to nature" *(para physin).* In this he appeals to a well-known condemnation of homoerotic behavior found both in Hellenistic Judaism and among Cynic-Stoic philosophers. See Robin Scroggs, *The New Testament and Homosexuality: Contextual Background for Contemporary Debate* (Philadelphia: Fortress, 1983), pp. 59-60; Richard B. Hays, "Relations Natural and Unnatural: A Response to John Boswell's Exegesis of Romans 1," *Journal of Religious Ethics* 14 (1986): 192-94.

⁴Kenneth J. Dover, *Greek Homosexuality* (London: Duckworth, 1978), p. 17. See Aline Rousselle, *Porneia: On Desire and the Body in Antiquity,* trans. Felicia Pheasant (1983; reprint Oxford: Basil Blackwell, 1988).

[5]Cf. Tobit 4:12; *Testament of Levi* 9:9-10. See O. Larry Yarbrough's in-depth study of 1 Thessalonians 4:3-8 and its relation with 1 Corinthians 7:2 in *Not like the Gentiles: Marriage Rules in the Letters of Paul,* Society of Biblical Literature Dissertation Series 80 (Atlanta: Scholars, 1985), pp. 65-87.

[6]Wayne A. Meeks, *The First Urban Christians: The Social World of the Apostle Paul* (New Haven, Conn.: Yale University Press, 1983), pp. 100-101.

[7]Gordon D. Fee, *God's Empowering Presence: The Holy Spirit in the Letters of Paul* (Peabody, Mass.: Hendrickson, 1994), pp. 124-25.

[8]Judith M. Gundry Volf, *Paul and Perseverance: Staying in and Falling Away* (Louisville, Ky.: Westminster/John Knox, 1990), pp. 117-18.

[9]This is a theme found also, for example, in the Cynic-Stoic literature, demonstrating that other thinkers of Paul's day found unbridled license to be a problem.

[10]The traditional interpretation of 1 Corinthians 7:1 is that it says the same thing as 7:7-8 and 38 in different words: "It is well for a man not to take a woman [as his wife]." However, many scholars and major translations place 7:1b in quotation marks, suggesting that Paul quotes austere Corinthians: "It is well for a man not to touch a woman." See William E. Phipps, "Is Paul's Attitude Toward Sexual Relations Contained in 1 Cor 7.1?" *New Testament Studies* 28 (1982): 125-31. There are no quotation marks in the original Greek, so the insertion of them is an interpretation or gloss that is not part of the text. This consensus needs to be challenged for the following reasons: (a) 7:7-8 ties in the chapter with Paul's literary strategy of arguing from personal example in every other topic in the letter; (b) Paul uses the same grammatical construction of 7:1b (*kalon* + dative + verb) in several other places, notably 7:8, 26 and 9:15 in the same letter, suggesting that 7:1b is Paul's thought expressed in Paul's language; (c) the way the chapter is introduced *(peri de)* is no longer able to be considered evidence that Paul cites a Corinthian phrase in 7:1, since "now concerning" may just as well introduce 7:1-24 or the entire chapter. See Margaret M. Mitchell, "Concerning *peri de* in 1 Corinthians," *Novum Testamentum* 31 (1989): 229-56.

[11]To quote an apt expression from a lecture by Donald Joy of Asbury Theological Seminary.

[12]John Boswell, *Christianity, Social Tolerance and Homosexuality: Gay People in Western Europe from the Beginning of the Christian Era to the Fourteenth Century* (Chicago: University of Chicago Press, 1980), pp. 91-117, 335-53. Boswell's influence has been disseminated by John J. McNeil *(The Church and the Homosexual* [Kansas City: Sheed, Andrews & McMeel, 1976], p. 200 n. 39), who, though publishing earlier than Boswell, has expressed his dependence on Boswell's ideas.

[13]See William L. Petersen, "Can *ARSENOKOITAI* Be Translated by 'Homosexuals'? (1 Cor 6:9; 1 Tim 1:10)," *Vigiliae Christianae* 40 (1986): 188-89.

[14]Dover, *Greek Homosexuality,* p. 1 n. 1.

[15]For this and a thorough refutation of Boswell's exegesis, see Hays, "Relations Natural and Unnatural."

[16]Scroggs, *New Testament and Homosexuality,* pp. 109-18.

[17]As Scroggs (ibid., pp. 66-98) is well aware.

[18]With the possible but unlikely exception of *Sibylline Oracles* 2.73, written sometime between B.C.E. 30 and C.E. 250, but probably later rather than earlier. See James H. Charlesworth, ed., *Apocalyptic Literature and Testaments,* vol. 1 of *The Old Testament Pseudepigrapha* (New York: Doubleday, 1983), p. 331.

[19]Translating the Hebrew for "lying with a male" *(miškāb zākûr);* Scroggs, *New Testament and Homosexuality,* pp. 106-8. Scroggs and David F. Wright ("Homosexuals or Prostitutes? The Meaning of ARSENOKOITAI [1 Cor. 6:9, 1 Tim. 1:10]," *Vigilae Christianae* 38 [1984]: 125-53) offer a convincing counter to Boswell's suggestion that *arsenokoitai* in 1 Corinthians 6:9 and 1 Timothy 1:10 refers to prostitution (*Christianity, Social Tolerance and Homosexuality,* pp. 341-44). Etymology, the deciphering of a term's meaning from its component parts, can be resorted to only when there is no evidence of the term's usage in the same period. Paul's usage of *arsenokoitai* is known as the earliest use of this term, which can be quickly demonstrated by a computer search of the known Greek literature in the *Thesaurus Linguae Graecae.* On linguistic cautions against using etymology to determine a term's meaning, see Peter Cotterell and Max Turner, *Linguistics and Biblical Interpretation* (Downers Grove, Ill.: InterVarsity Press/London: S.P.C.K., 1989), pp. 129-83.

[20]Scroggs, "Appendix A: On the Question of Nonpederastic Male Homosexuality," in *New Testament and Homosexuality,* pp. 130-39.

[21]Ibid., p. 133.

[22]See his disclaimer on p. 139!

[23]The upshot of Scroggs, *New Testament and Homosexuality.*

[24]Current initiatives to change the *legal* definition of marriage in some Western societies does not affect this biblical argument. In response to a suit brought by three gay couples, the high court of Hawaii recently ruled that barring homosexual marriage is sex-discriminatory. However, the court did not overturn state law, which would have forced all fifty states to recognize Hawaii's gay and lesbian marriages. Many places settle for a definition of "domestic partnerships," which grant the same benefits to the cohabiting partners of employees as are granted to spouses (such as health care insurance).

[25]See Rousselle, *Porneia,* pp. 24-46.

[26]Scroggs, *New Testament and Homosexuality,* p. 117.

[27]Hays, "Relations Natural and Unnatural," pp. 189-91, 210.

[28]See A. P. Bell and M. S. Weinberg, *Homosexualities: A Study of Diversity Among Men and Women* (New York: Simon & Schuster, 1978).

[29]Cited in Stanton L. Jones, *The Gay Debate* (Downers Grove, Ill.: InterVarsity Press, 1994), pp. 17-18.

[30]See Victor Paul Furnish, *The Moral Teaching of Paul* (Nashville: Abingdon, 1979), pp. 52-83.

[31]Victor Paul Furnish, "The Bible and Homosexuality: Reading the Texts in Context," in *Homosexuality in the Church: Both Sides of the Debate,* ed. Jeffrey S. Siker (Louisville, Ky.: Westminster/John Knox, 1994), p. 24.

[32]James D. G. Dunn, *Romans 1—8,* Word Biblical Commentary 38A (Dallas: Word, 1988), p. 74. John Ziesler *(Paul's Letter to the Romans* [London: SCM Press, 1989], p. 78), however, thinks it "may refer to sexually transmitted disease" but "most likely" to perversion as its own penalty.

[33]C. E. B. Cranfield, *A Critical and Exegetical Commentary on the Epistle to the Romans,* International Critical Commentary (Edinburgh: T & T Clark, 1975), 1:126-27.

Chapter 4: Single Paul & His Married Followers

[1]Martin Dibelius and Werner Georg Kümmel *(Paul,* trans. Franke Clarke [Philadelphia: Westminster Press, 1953], pp. 35-36) think that Paul's ambivalence about marriage in 1 Corinthians 7 demonstrates that he had no personal experience, that he was a bachelor and not a widower. I find this to be the most likely view, but it cannot be confirmed from the text.

[2]Robert Jewett, *Paul, the Apostle to America: Cultural Trends and Pauline Scholarship* (Louisville, Ky.: Westminster/John Knox, 1994), p. 18. Strangely, in a book that harshly castigates New Testament scholarship for its bondage to European conventions, Jewett never acknowledges that this key operating principle of his interpretation of Paul is very European, one of the heaviest influences of Continental scholarship on current Pauline studies.

[3]Luke Timothy Johnson, *The Writings of the New Testament: An Interpretation* (Philadelphia: Fortress, 1986), pp. 255-57.

[4]Jewett, *Paul, the Apostle to America,* pp. 53, 64.

[5]For example, Eduard Schweizer, *The Letter to the Colossians,* trans. Andrew Chester (1976; reprint Minneapolis: Augsburg, 1982), pp. 15-24.

[6]See Clinton E. Arnold, "Letter to the Ephesians," in *Dictionary of Paul and His Letters,* ed. Gerald F. Hawthorne, Ralph P. Martin and Daniel G. Reid (Downers Grove, Ill.: InterVarsity Press, 1993).

[7]See J. Christiaan Beker, *Heirs of Paul: Paul's Legacy in the New Testament and in*

the Church Today (Minneapolis: Augsburg, 1991).

[8]In an otherwise highly nuanced account, Jewett *(Paul, the Apostle to America,* p. 64) makes too simplistic and too sharp a disjunction between Colossians on the one hand and 1 Corinthians and Philemon on the other.

[9]Abraham J. Malherbe, "Hellenistic Moralists and the New Testament," in *Aufstieg und Niedergang der Römischen Welt,* ed. H. Temporini (Berlin: De Gruyter, 1992), 2.26.1, p. 311 n. 214.

[10]Wayne A. Meeks, *The Moral World of the First Christians* (London: S.P.C.K., 1986), p. 113.

[11]David L. Balch, *Let Wives Be Submissive: The Domestic Code in 1 Peter,* Society of Biblical Literature Monograph Series 26 (Atlanta: Scholars, 1981), pp. 81-116.

[12]As argued by Craig S. Keener in *Paul, Women and Wives: Marriage and Women's Ministry in the Letters of Paul* (Peabody, Mass.: Hendrickson, 1992), pp. 139-56.

[13]Andrew T. Lincoln, *Paradise Now and Not Yet,* Society for New Testament Studies Monograph Series 43 (Cambridge: Cambridge University Press, 1981), pp. 130-34.

[14]Andrew T. Lincoln, *Ephesians,* Word Biblical Commentary 42 (Dallas: Word, 1990), pp. 358-65.

[15]Aristotle *Politics* 1.1253b.

[16]Philo *Hypothetica* 8.7.14.

[17]Josephus *Against Apion* 2.201.

[18]Translation in Balch, *Let Wives Be Submissive,* p. 42 (see his many other examples, pp. 33-59); Yarbrough, *Not like the Gentiles,* pp. 53-57; Keener, *Paul, Women and Wives,* pp. 159-66.

[19]What follows are the views, respectively, of Stephen B. Clark (*Man and Woman in Christ* [Ann Arbor, Mich.: Servant, 1980], pp. 71-87) and J. Paul Sampley (*"And the Two Shall Become One Flesh": A Study of Traditions in Ephesians 5:21-33* [Cambridge: Cambridge University Press, 1971]).

[20]Keener, *Paul, Women and Wives,* p. 158.

[21]See Lincoln, *Ephesians,* pp. 365-66.

[22]Elisabeth Schüssler Fiorenza, *In Memory of Her: A Feminist Theological Reconstruction of Christian Origins* (New York: Crossroad, 1983), p. 269.

[23]Ibid.

[24]Jewett ("The Sexual Liberation of Paul and His Churches," in *Paul, the Apostle to America,* pp. 45-58) insightfully argues that Paul's experience of "sexual liberation" (Prisca as a leader, for example) probably preceded his theorizing about it and that we can sense both a tension and a development in Paul on the matter. The suggestion is a helpful one, even if we disagree with the specifics of the speculative way Jewett develops his argument.

[25]As Lincoln (*Ephesians,* pp. 367-68) points out, the difference is not so much between submission and obedience as between willfully choosing to be subordinate and being forced to obey.

[26]Keener, *Paul, Women and Wives,* p. 207. See his "A Model for Interpreting Wives' Submission—Slaves in Ephesians 6:5-9," pp. 184-224, where this hermeneutical point is argued at length.

[27]An expression attributed to Sir Richard Burton, Victorian explorer and translator of the Kamasutra (Janet Daley, "Death of the Seventh Commandment?" *London Sunday Times,* March 26, 1995, p. 11).

[28]Divorce and remarriage are not treated here as a "problem of Paul," for these are issues that the Bible as a whole presents. For an excellent and sensitive treatment of this important and challenging issue, see Craig S. Keener, *And Marries Another: Divorce and Remarriage in the Teaching of the New Testament* (Peabody, Mass.: Hendrickson, 1991).

[29]Hyam Maccoby, *The Mythmaker: Paul and the Invention of Christianity* (New York: Harper & Row, 1986), p. 199.

[30]Karl Olav Sandnes, *Paul—One of the Prophets? A Contribution to the Apostle's Self-Understanding,* Wissenschaftliche Untersuchungen zum Neuen Testament 2/43 (Tübingen: J. C. B. Mohr [Paul Siebeck], 1991), pp. 6-7.

[31]See the collection of classic articles by Jerome Murphy-O'Connor and James H. Charlesworth, eds., *Paul and the Dead Sea Scrolls* (1968; reprint New York: Crossroad, 1990).

[32]Epictetus *Discourses* 3.22.47.

[33]Ibid., 3.22.67-76.

[34]I am guessing that single parents (particularly of younger children) have even less time than married couples to devote to Christian service. Paul's comments are directed to those who are unmarried without children.

Chapter 5: The Slave of Christ & the Slaves of Antiquity

[1]Caroline Lees and Simon Hinde, "Scandal of Football's Child Slavery," *London Sunday Times,* May 14, 1995, p. 6.

[2]Here, as for much of this chapter, I am dependent on S. Scott Bartchy, *First-Century Slavery and 1 Corinthians 7:21,* Society of Biblical Literature Dissertation Series 11 (Atlanta: Scholars, 1973), pp. 63-64, 116-17.

[3]One suspects that predominantly American translations of the Bible, influenced by guilt and shame from the recent past, have unconsciously attempted to make the Bible appear less offensive. See Walter Bauer, William F. Arndt, F. Wilbur Gingrich and Frederick W. Danker, *A Greek-English Lexicon of the New Testament and Other*

Early Christian Literature (original ed. 1957; rev. ed. Chicago: University of Chicago Press, 1979), p. 205.

⁴The Old Testament passages on slavery are not any more promising, since the manumission rules applied to Hebrews and not foreigners (cf. Ex 21:2-11, 20-21, 26-27; Lev 25:39-55; Deut 15:12-18; 21:10-14; 23:15-16). Slavery was an almost universally accepted social fact in antiquity.

⁵Bartchy, *First-Century Slavery*, p. 68.

⁶Tiro obviously had written the letter as Cicero's secretary.

⁷Cicero *Correspondence with Family and Friends* 16.16 (as translated by Jo Ann Shelton, *As the Romans Did: A Sourcebook in Roman Social History* [Oxford: Oxford University Press, 1988], pp. 192-93).

⁸Columella *On Agriculture* 1.8.1-2 (as translated by Shelton, *As the Romans Did*, p. 171).

⁹See P. R. C. Weaver, *FAMILIA CAESARIS: A Social Study of the Emperor's Freedmen and Slaves* (Cambridge: Cambridge University Press, 1972).

¹⁰Weaver, "Age at Manumission," in *FAMILIA CAESARIS*, pp. 97-104.

¹¹Epictetus *Dissertations* 4.1.37.

¹²Seneca the Younger *Letters* 47 (as translated by Shelton, *As the Romans Did*, p. 186).

¹³Seneca *De ira* 3.40; *Dio Cassius* 54.23.

¹⁴A metaphor that was a commonplace of Hellenistic moral philosophy (Epictetus *Dissertations* 4.1; 2.123) and Hellenistic Judaism (Philo *Quod Omnis Probus Liber Sit* 21-25, 156-59).

¹⁵Edwin A. Judge, *The Social Pattern of the Christian Groups in the First Century* (London: Tyndale, 1960), p. 38.

¹⁶Second Corinthians 4:5; cf. 2 Corinthians 2:14; 3:6; 1 Corinthians 3:5. David M. Stanley ("Imitation in Paul's Letters: Its Significance for His Relationship to Jesus and His Own Christian Foundations," in *From Jesus to Paul: Studies in Honour of Francis Wright Beare*, ed. P. Richardson and J. Hurd [Waterloo, Ont.: Wilfred Laurier University Press, 1984], pp. 131) calls this "the most revealing metaphor" of Paul's relationship with Christ.

¹⁷Francis Lyall, *Slaves, Citizens, Sons: Legal Metaphors in the Epistles* (Grand Rapids, Mich.: Academie/Zondervan, 1984), p. 39; see especially pp. 19-46 for a very readable treatment of the conditions of slavery and emancipation in Paul's day.

¹⁸For a more detailed analysis of the relationship of Galatians 1:10 with the rest of the letter, see my "Christ's Slave, People Pleasers and Galatians 1:10," *New Testament Studies* 42 (1996): 90-104.

¹⁹See James D. G. Dunn, *The Epistle to the Galatians*, Black's New Testament Commentary (London: A & C Black, 1993), p. 51.

[20]See Weaver, *FAMILIA CAESARIS;* Demetrius J. Kyrtatas, "Christianity and the Familia Caesaris," in *The Social Structure of the Early Christian Communities* (London: Verso, 1987), pp. 75-86; Dale B. Martin, *Slavery as Salvation: The Metaphor of Slavery in Pauline Christianity* (New Haven, Conn.: Yale University Press, 1990), pp. 1-49.

[21]Deuteronomy 34:5; Joshua 1:1, 13, 15; 8:31, 33; 11:12; 12:6; 13:8; 14:7; 18:7; 22:2, 4, 5; 24:29; Judges 2:8; 2 Kings 18:12; 2 Chronicles 1:3; 24:6; Psalms 18:1; 36:1; Isaiah 42:19.

[22]Karl Olav Sandnes, *Paul—One of the Prophets? A Contribution to the Apostle's Self-Understanding,* Wissenschaftliche Untersuchungen zum Neuen Testament 2/43 (Tübingen: J. C. B. Mohr [Paul Siebeck], 1991), pp. 59-65, 147-48.

[23]Cf. Galatians 1:10; 2:4-5; 3:23; 3:29—4:9; 4:21—5:1; 5:13; LXX Jeremiah 2:14, 20; 3:22; 5:19; 8:2; 10:24; 11:10; 13:10; 15:14; 16:11, 13; 22:9; 25:6, 11; 34:6; 41:9, 13; 42:15; 43:31; 44:2, 18.

[24]Martin, *Slavery as Salvation,* pp. 50-85.

[25]Galatians 2:4; 3:28; 4:1, 3, 7, 8, 9, 22-23, 24, 25; 5:1, 13; cf. also the redemption language (3:13; 4:5), the frequency of *free* and *freedom,* and the imprisonment imagery (3:22-23).

[26]Romans 1:1; 7:25; 11:13; 15:16, 25, 27, 31; 1 Corinthians 3:5; 4:1-2; 7:22; 9:16-23, 27; 2 Corinthians 2:14; 3:3, 6-9; 4:1, 5; 5:14, 18; 6:3-4; 8:4, 19, 20; 9:1, 12; 13; 11:8, 15, 23; 12:10; Galatians 1:10; Philippians 1:1, 7, 13, 14, 17; Philemon 1, 9, 10, 13.

[27]Peter Marshall, "A Metaphor of Social Shame: *THRIAMBEUEIN* in 2 Cor 2:14," *Novum Testamentum* 25 (1983): 302-17.

[28]Heinz Schreckenberg, *ANANKE, Untersuchungen zur Geschichte des Wortgebrauchs,* Zetemata 36 (Munich: Beck'sche, 1964), pp. 1-36, 49-54.

[29]Martin, *Slavery as Salvation,* pp. 117-35.

[30]Cf. John 15:13-15, where Jesus calls the disciples friends instead of slaves.

[31]Cited in Shelton, *As the Romans Did,* pp. 193-94.

[32]Henry Chadwick, *The Early Church* (Baltimore: Penguin, 1967), pp. 59-60.

[33]Jewett, *Paul, the Apostle to America,* pp. 59-69.

[34]James L. Bailey and Lyle D. Vander Broek, *Literary Forms in the New Testament* (London: S.P.C.K., 1992), p. 70.

[35]See Bartchy, *First-Century Slavery,* pp. 114-20.

[36]Norman Petersen, *Rediscovering Paul: Philemon and the Sociology of Paul's Narrative World* (Philadelphia: Fortress, 1985), pp. 43-88. For an outline of the full "story," see pp. 69-71.

[37]Defended recently by J. G. Nordling, "*Onesimus Fugitivus:* A Defense of the Runaway Slave Hypothesis in Philemon," *Journal for the Study of the New Testament* 41

(1991): 97-119. He does not consider Lampe's view, adopted here.

[38]Peter Lampe, "Keine 'Sklavenflucht' des Onesimus," *Zeitschrift für die neuetestamentliche Wissenschaft* 76 (1985): 135-37; followed by S. Scott Bartchy, "Philemon, Epistle to," in *Anchor Bible Dictionary,* ed. David N. Freedman (New York: Doubleday, 1992), 5:305-10; Arthur G. Patzia, "Philemon, Letter to," in *Dictionary of Paul and His Letters,* ed. Gerald F. Hawthorne, Ralph P. Martin and Daniel G. Reid (Downers Grove, Ill.: InterVarsity Press, 1993), pp. 703-7, and developed by Brian M. Rapske, "The Prisoner Paul in the Eyes of Onesimus," *New Testament Studies* 37 (1991): 187-203.

[39]C. F. D. Moule (*The Epistles to the Colossians and to Philemon,* Cambridge Greek Testament Commentary [Cambridge: Cambridge University Press, 1962]) notes that this theory must suppose that Paul's imprisonment "was of a lax sort" suggested by Acts 24:23; 28:16, 30. But even in these cases Paul remained under the supervision of a centurion or soldier who presumably would be compelled to uphold the law. For the legal obligations, see Nordling, *"Onesimus Fugitivus,"* pp. 114-17, who overlooks the difficulties these obligations raise for the runaway theory.

[40]Sarah C. Winter, "Paul's Letter to Philemon," *New Testament Studies* 33 (1987): 2. Some, but not all, temples had the right of asylum (Moule, *Epistles to the Colossians and to Philemon,* p. 37).

[41]Bartchy, "Philemon," p. 307.

[42]We should reject the other recent hypothesis that Philemon sent Onesimus to Paul (suggested in J. L. Houlden, *Paul's Letters from Prison: Philippians, Colossians, Philemon and Ephesians* [Philadelphia: Westminster Press, 1970], p. 226; developed by Winter, "Paul's Letter to Philemon," and followed by Wolfgang Schenk, "Der Brief des Paulus an Philemon in der neueren Forschung [1945—1987]," *Aufstieg und Niedergang der römischen Welt* [Berlin: Walter De Gruyter, 1987], 2.25.4, pp. 3439-95). Philemon 13 cannot be taken as support for this view, since the "in order that" clause suggests that Philemon's vicarious "ministry" through Onesimus would come as a *result* of Paul's retention of the slave rather than Philemon's *previous* design, as Paul elaborates in verse 14.

[43]If Onesimus were in fact a runaway, he could be whipped, imprisoned and even crucified according to the Oxyrhynchus Papyrus 1643 (cited in Ralph P. Martin, *Ephesians, Colossians and Philemon* [Atlanta: John Knox, 1991], p. 136). If this was the case, Paul's appeal was for clemency.

[44]Eduard Lohse, *Colossians and Philemon,* Hermeneia (Philadelphia: Fortress, 1971), p. 187.

[45]The Oxyrhynchus Papyrus 1422 "contains a notice that persons who gave shelter to escaped slaves were to be held accountable in law and could be prosecuted by the slaves' master" (Ralph P. Martin, *Colossians and Philemon* New Century Bible [Lon-

don: Marshall, Morgan & Scott, 1973], p. 167).

[46]Martin, *Ephesians, Colossians and Philemon,* p. 144.

[47]Petersen, *Rediscovering Paul,* p. 105.

[48]For example, Ernst Lohmeyer, *Die Briefe an die Philipper, an die Kolosser und an Philemon* (1930; reprint Göttingen, Germany: Vandenhoeck & Ruprecht, 1964), p. 191.

[49]Martin, *Ephesians, Colossians and Philemon,* pp. 142, 145.

[50]Bartchy, "Philemon," p. 309.

[51]Théo Preiss, *Life in Christ,* trans. Harold Knight, Studies in Biblical Theology 13 (Chicago: Allenson, 1954), pp. 32-42; Ernest Best, *One Body in Christ: A Study in the Relationship of the Church to Christ in the Epistles of the Apostle Paul* (London: S.P.C.K., 1955), pp. 1-33.

[52]For example, 1 Corinthians 7; 2 Corinthians 8.

[53]Petersen, *Rediscovering Paul,* p. 132.

[54]F. Forrester Church, "Rhetorical Structure and Design in Paul's Letter to Philemon," *Harvard Theological Review* 71 (1978): 24-25.

[55]John L. White, "The Structural Analysis of Philemon: A Point of Departure in the Formal Analysis of the Pauline Letter," *Society of Biblical Literature Seminar Papers,* 1971, pp. 35-36.

[56]John Knox, *Philemon Among the Letters of Paul* (London: Collins, 1960), p. 20.

[57]So Carl Bjerkelund, *Parakalô: Form, Funktion und Sinn der parakalô-Sätze in den paulinischen Briefen* (Oslo: Universitetsforlaget, 1967), pp. 120-22.

[58]John M. G. Barclay, "Paul, Philemon and the Dilemma of Christian Slave-Ownership," *New Testament Studies* 37 (1991): 161-86.

[59]Bartchy, *First-Century Slavery,* pp. 88-91.

[60]John H. Elliott, "Patronage and Clientism in Early Christian Society," *Forum* 31 (1987): 39-48.

[61]Petersen, *Rediscovering Paul,* p. 289.

[62]Cf. John H. Elliott, "Philemon and House Churches," *The Bible Today* 22 (1984): 145-50; Bartchy, "Philemon," p. 308-9.

[63]Bartchy, "Slavery (Greco-Roman)," p. 70.

[64]Church, "Rhetorical Structure and Design," pp. 22-24, 27.

[65]Mary Ann Getty, "The Theology of Philemon," *Society of Biblical Literature Seminar Papers* 26 (1987): 504.

[66]N. T. Wright, *The Epistles of Paul to the Colossians and to Philemon,* Tyndale New Testament Commentary (Leicester, England: Inter-Varsity Press, 1986), pp. 175-78.

[67]Does Paul's expressed desire for freedom (v. 22) give Philemon food for thought about Onesimus's future?

[68]For the references to Clement, Ignatius and Hermas I am indebted to Bartchy, *First-Century Slavery*, pp. 100-101, but the translations come from J. B. Lightfoot and J. R. Harmer, *The Apostolic Fathers*, 2nd ed., ed. and rev. Michael W. Holmes (Grand Rapids, Mich.: Baker Book House, 1989).

[69]Ignatius *To Polycarp* 4.3.

[70]Shepherd of Hermas; *Mandate* 8.10; *Similitude* 1.10.

Chapter 6: The Hebrew of Hebrews & Anti-Semitism

[1]Irvin J. Borowsky, foreword to *Jews and Christians: Exploring the Past, Present and Future*, ed. James H. Charlesworth (New York: Crossroad, 1990), p. 9.

[2]For a good overview of the issues and a careful treatment of the texts, see Craig A. Evans and Donald A. Hagner, eds., *Anti-Semitism and Early Christianity: Issues of Polemic and Faith* (Minneapolis: Fortress, 1993); P. Richardson and D. Granskou, eds., *Paul and the Gospels*, vol. 1 of *Anti-Judaism in Early Christianity* (Waterloo, Ont.: Wilfred Laurier University Press, 1986).

[3]Sydney G. Hall III, *Christian Anti-Semitism and Paul's Theology* (Minneapolis: Fortress, 1993), p. 156 n. 11.

[4]For example, W. D. Davies, "Paul and the People of Israel," *New Testament Studies* 24 (1977-1978): 18; James D. G. Dunn, "Echoes of Intra-Jewish Polemic in Paul's Letter to the Galatians," *Journal of Biblical Literature* 112 (1993): 459-77.

[5]See, for example, Karl-Wilhelm Niebuhr, *Heidenapostel aus Israel: Die jüdische Identität des Paulus nach ihrer Darstellung in seinen Briefen*, Wissenschaftliche Untersuchungen zum Neuen Testament 62 (Tübingen: J. C. B. Mohr [Paul Siebeck], 1992).

[6]See Claudia Setzer, *Jewish Responses to Early Christians: History and Polemics, 30-150 C.E.* (Minneapolis: Fortress, 1994).

[7]See Francis Watson, *Paul, Judaism and the Gentiles: A Sociological Approach* (Cambridge: Cambridge University Press, 1986).

[8]See John T. Fitzgerald, *Cracks in an Earthen Vessel: An Examination of the Catalogues of Hardships in the Corinthian Correspondence*, Society of Biblical Literature Dissertation Series 99 (Atlanta: Scholars, 1988), p. 42; Martin Ebner, *Leidenlisten und Apostelbrief: Untersuchungen zu Form, Motivik und Funktion der Peristasenkataloge bei Paulus* (Würzburg, Germany: Echter, 1991), pp. 93-172.

[9]Epictetus *Dissertationes* 1.24.1.

[10]So, for example, E. P. Sanders, "Paul on the Law, His Opponents and the Jewish People in Philippians 3 and 2 Corinthians 11," in *Paul and the Gospels*, vol. 1 of *Anti-Judaism in Early Christianity* (Waterloo, Ont.: Wilfred Laurier University Press, 1986), pp. 83-84—against, for example, A. F. J. Klijn, "Paul's Opponents in Philippians 3," *Novum Testamentum* 7 (1964): 278-84; Gerald F. Hawthorne, *Philippians*,

Word Biblical Commentary 43 (Waco, Tex.: Word, 1983), pp. xliv-xlvii.

[11]Ralph P. Martin, *Philippians,* New Century Bible (1976; reprint Grand Rapids, Mich.: Eerdmans, 1980), p. 125.

[12]Kenneth Grayston, "The Opponents in Philippians 3," *Expository Times* 97 (1986): 171; Joachim Gnilka, *Der Philipperbrief,* Herder Theologische Kommentar (Freiburg, Germany: Herder, 1968), pp. 186-87.

[13]So, for example, Sanders, "Paul on the Law," pp. 83-84; Joseph B. Tyson, "Paul's Opponents at Philippi," *Perspectives in Religious Studies* 3 (1976): 82-95.

[14]Cf. Jean-François Collange, *The Epistle of Saint Paul to the Philippians,* trans. A. W. Heathcote (London: Epworth, 1979), pp. 136-37.

[15]Helmut Koester, "The Purpose of the Polemic of a Pauline Fragment (Philippians 3)," *New Testament Studies* 8 (1961-1962): 326-27; John J. Gunther, *St. Paul's Opponents and Their Background: A Study of Apocalyptic and Jewish Sectarian Teachings,* Supplements to *Novum Testamentum* 35 (Leiden: Brill, 1973), p. 98; William S. Kurz, "Kenotic Imitation of Paul and of Christ in Philippians 2 and 3," in *Discipleship in the New Testament,* ed. Fernando F. Segovia (Philadelphia: Fortress, 1985), pp. 116.

[16]Christopher Mearns, "The Identity of Paul's Opponents at Philippi," *New Testament Studies* 33 (1987): 198-200.

[17]"Dogs" (Phil 3:2) cannot be appealed to as a libertine epithet, because it is just as likely an ironical turn of phrase against Jewish opponents; contra Walter Schmithals, "The False Teachers of the Epistle to the Philippians," in *Paul and the Gnostics,* trans. John E. Steely (Nashville: Abingdon, 1972), pp. 84-85.

[18]Ibid., p. 109.

[19]Robert Jewett, "Conflicting Movements in the Early Church as Reflected in Philippians," *Novum Testamentum* 12 (1970): 379-80; Martin, *Philippians,* pp. 145-46.

[20]The most commonly cited article is Birger Pearson, "1 Thessalonians 2:13-16: A Deutero-Pauline Interpolation," *Harvard Theological Review* 64 (1971): 79-91.

[21]For arguments against the interpolation theory, see, for example, Donald A. Hagner, "Paul's Quarrel with Judaism," in *Anti-Semitism and Early Christianity: Issues of Polemic and Faith,* ed. Craig A. Evans and Donald A. Hagner (Minneapolis: Fortress, 1993), pp. 130-33.

[22]Ibid., p. 134.

[23]See Mary C. Callaway, "A Hammer That Breaks Rock in Pieces: Prophetic Critique in the Hebrew Bible," in *Anti-Semitism and Early Christianity: Issues of Polemic and Faith,* ed. Craig A. Evans and Donald A. Hagner (Minneapolis: Fortress, 1993), pp. 21-38.

[24]Luke Timothy Johnson, "The New Testament's Anti-Jewish Slander and the Conventions of Ancient Polemic," *Journal of Biblical Literature* 108 (1989): 429. For this reference I am dependent on Hagner, "Paul's Quarrel with Judaism," p. 134 n. 27.

[25]The difficulty posed by Paul's general usage of the accepted ancient practice of polemic will be addressed in the next chapter.

[26]Hall, *Christian Anti-Semitism and Paul's Theology,* pp. 40-41.

[27]This excerpt from Luther's *Works* comes from Hall, *Christian Anti-Semitism and Paul's Theology,* pp. 45-46.

[28]Hans J. Hillerbrand, "Martin Luther and the Jews," in *Jews and Christians: Exploring the Past, Present and Future,* ed. James H. Charlesworth (New York: Crossroad, 1990), p. 149.

[29]The flagship for this new understanding is E. P. Sanders, *Paul and Palestinian Judaism: A Comparison of Patterns of Religion* (Minneapolis: Fortress, 1977). On the initial impact of Sanders's contribution to Pauline studies, see the seminal article by James D. G. Dunn, "The New Perspective on Paul," *Bulletin of the John Rylands Library* 65 (1983): 95-122, reprinted with additional comments in *Jesus, Paul and the Law: Studies in Mark and Galatians* (Louisville, Ky.: Westminster/John Knox, 1990), pp. 183-214. For an overview of this recent development of Pauline interpretation in light of its historical antecedents, see Scott J. Hafemann, "Paul and His Interpreters," in *Dictionary of Paul and His Letters,* ed. Gerald F. Hawthorne, Ralph P. Martin and Daniel G. Reid (Downers Grove, Ill.: InterVarsity Press, 1993), pp. 666-79.

[30]See Krister Stendahl, *Paul Among Jews and Gentiles* (Philadelphia: Fortress, 1976).

[31]Even though I find several things to disagree with, Clark M. Williamson and Ronald J. Allen *(Interpreting Difficult Texts: Anti-Judaism and Christian Preaching* [London: SCM Press/Trinity, 1989]) have wrestled with the issue for Christian preaching, and their book helps sensitize us to the wrongful offense caused by a caricatured use of *Jews* and *Judaism.*

[32]See n. 29.

[33]For a readable and up-to-date treatment of the complicated issue of Paul's attitude toward the law, see Frank Thielman, *Paul and the Law: A Contextual Approach* (Downers Grove, Ill.: InterVarsity Press, 1994).

[34]Hagner, "Paul's Quarrel with Judaism," p. 129.

[35]See Jacob M. Myers and Edwin D. Freed, "Is Paul Also Among the Prophets?" *Interpretation* 20 (1966): 40-53; Sandnes, *Paul—One of the Prophets?*

[36]See Ben Witherington III, *Paul's Narrative Thought World: The Tapestry of Tragedy and Triumph* (Louisville, Ky.: Westminster/John Knox, 1994).

[37]On the difference between allusion and citation in Paul and his way of citing the Old Testament, see Christopher D. Stanley, *Paul and the Language of Scripture: Citation Technique in the Pauline Epistles and Contemporary Literature,* Society for New Testament Studies Monograph Series 74 (Cambridge: Cambridge University Press, 1992); Richard B. Hays, *Echoes of Scripture in the Letters of Paul* (New Haven, Conn.: Yale University Press, 1989); and E. Earl Ellis, *Paul's Use of the Old Testament*

(1957; reprint Grand Rapids, Mich.: Baker Book House, 1981).

[38]Hagner, "Paul's Quarrel with Judaism," pp. 144-45.

[39]See Moisés Silva, "Old Testament in Paul," in *Dictionary of Paul and His Letters,* ed. Gerald F. Hawthorne, Ralph P. Martin and Daniel G. Reid (Downers Grove, Ill.: InterVarsity Press, 1993), pp. 630-42.

[40]Many scholars are quick to draw attention not to Paul's complex and sophisticated way of arguing, but to the differences between chapters 8 and 10. For a survey of the issues, see W. Wendell Willis, *Idol Meat in Corinth: The Pauline Argument in 1 Corinthians 8 and 10,* Society of Biblical Literature Dissertation Series 68 (Chico, Calif.: Scholars, 1985). The difficulty with this sort of approach is that it leaves out the obvious literary device of chapter 9, which fits between chapters 8 and 10 in a way analogous to how 1 Corinthians 13 functions between chapters 12 and 14. In response to this cut-and-paste approach, Peter D. Gooch (*Dangerous Food: 1 Corinthians 8—10 in Its Context,* Studies in Christianity and Judaism 5 [Waterloo, Ont.: Wilfred Laurier University Press, 1993]), following John C. Hurd, offers an interpretation that takes 1 Corinthians 8—10 as a whole in light of the Corinthian social setting.

[41]"The weaker brothers" could be Jewish, or they could be Gentiles who would be tempted to return to their former practice of idolatry, which they left to join the Christian community (1 Cor 8:7).

[42]A surface comparison of Romans 7 and 2 Corinthians 3 immediately reveals how complicated this question is; it also displays how passionately Paul wrestled with the continuing place of the law for the Christian. For the hardier Bible student, a study of the law in Romans will prove the point. For a review of the issues, see Frank Thielman, "Law," in *Dictionary of Paul and His Letters,* ed. Gerald F. Hawthorne, Ralph P. Martin and Daniel G. Reid (Downers Grove, Ill.: InterVarsity Press, 1993), pp. 529-42; and his full-length *Paul and the Law.*

[43]See Victor P. Pfitzner, *Paul and the Agon Motif: Traditional Athletic Imagery in the Pauline Literature,* Supplements to Novum Testamentum 16 (Leiden: Brill, 1967), pp. 82-109.

[44]Illyricum is due east of Rome, across the Adriatic Sea.

[45]So F. F. Bruce, "The Romans Debate—Continued," in *The Romans Debate,* rev. ed., ed. K. P. Donfried (Edinburgh: T & T Clark, 1991), pp. 188-93.

[46]Dieter Georgi, *Remembering the Poor: The History of Paul's Collection for Jerusalem,* trans. I. Racz (1965; reprint Nashville: Abingdon, 1992), pp. 117-20.

[47]Horst Balz, "λειτουργέω κτλ.," *Exegetical Dictionary of the New Testament,* ed. Horst Balz and Gerhard Schneider (Grand Rapids, Mich.: Eerdmans, 1991), 2:347-49; James D. G. Dunn, *Romans 9—16,* Word Biblical Commentary 38B (Waco, Tex.: Word, 1988), pp. 859-60. It should not be overlooked that *leitourgia* was a common term for

the performance of Greek civic duty in antiquity, a usage not absent from Romans (13:6). But the Old Testament sense is clearly in view in Romans 15:16.

[48]Johannes Munck, *Paul and the Salvation of Mankind,* trans. Frank Clarke (1954; reprint London: SCM Press, 1959), pp. 49-50.

[49]A whole chapter could be devoted to Paul's perplexing interaction with the Colossian heresy, which seems to be based, at least partially, on a syncretistic, ascetic tendency of Judaism in the Lycus Valley of Asia Minor. The teaching Paul confronts combines Jewish and Hellenistic elements (Col 1:19, 25; 2:2, 3, 8, 9, 11-13, 16, 20, 21, 23; 4:17). See Peter T. O'Brien, *Colossians, Philemon,* Word Biblical Commentary 44 (Waco, Tex.: Word, 1982), pp. xxx-xli. Again, a discussion of Titus 1:10-16 could fill many more pages. See Knight, *Pastoral Epistles,* pp. 11-12, 295-304.

[50]See Romans 1:5, 13; 11:11-13, 25; 15:9, 16, 18, 27; cf. 16:26. Cf. Jürgen Becker, *Paul: Apostle to the Gentiles,* trans. O. C. Dean Jr. (Louisville, Ky.: Westminster/John Knox, 1993).

[51]For a reconstruction that emphasizes the continuity of Christianity and Judaism, arguing that the cleft developed more slowly than is often believed, see James D. G. Dunn, *The Partings of the Ways Between Christianity and Judaism* (London: SCM Press, 1991). On the other hand, see two Jewish writers who place the blame for the breach between Christianity and Judaism on Paul's shoulders. A moderate and balanced exegetical work is Alan F. Segal, *Paul the Convert: The Apostolate and Apostasy of Saul the Pharisee* (New Haven, Conn.: Yale University Press, 1990), which stands in contrast to the sensational and tendentious work by Hyam Maccoby, *The Mythmaker: Paul and the Invention of Christianity* (New York: Harper & Row, 1986).

[52]James D. G. Dunn, *The Epistle to the Galatians,* Black's New Testament Commentaries (London: A & C Black, 1993), p. 57. Dunn does not believe that Galatians 1:13-14 sets Christianity against Judaism. If he is right, then the next contrast between the two is in the second century: Ignatius *Letter to the Magnesians* 10.3 and *Letter to the Philadelphians* 6.1.

[53]Some scholars assert that Paul conceived of two ways of salvation: one through the law for Jews and another through faith in Christ for the Gentiles (for example, John Gager, *The Origins of Anti-Semitism: Attitudes Toward Judaism in Pagan and Christian Antiquity* [New York: Oxford University Press, 1983]; Lloyd Gaston, *Paul and the Torah* [Vancouver: University of British Columbia Press, 1987]; Hall, *Christian Anti-Semitism and Paul's Theology).* This approach overlooks the centrality of Christ for Paul's view of salvation and is undermined, for example, by 1 Corinthians 1:22-25 and 9:19-23, and the most straightforward reading of Romans 11:13-36 (especially 11:23). See, for example, E. P. Sanders, *Paul, the Law and the Jewish People* (Philadelphia: Fortress, 1983), pp. 170-74; Segal, *Paul the Convert,* pp. 279-84.

[54]Hans Hübner, *Gottes Ich und Israel: Zum Schriftgebrauch des Paulus in Römer 9— 11* (Göttingen, Germany: Vandenhoeck & Ruprecht, 1984), pp. 100-101.

[55]Johannes Munck, *Christ and Israel: An Interpretation of Romans 9—11,* trans. I. Nixon (Philadelphia: Fortress, 1967), pp. 104-43.

[56]The expression "all Israel will be saved" in Romans 11:26 must be interpreted in light of what has come before it in verse 23. That is, all Israel, the true people of God, will be saved through faith in Christ.

Chapter 7: Paul's Problem Personality

[1]Renan, cited in Malcolm Muggeridge and Alec Vidler, *Paul, Envoy Extraordinary* (London: Collins, 1972), p. 11.

[2]"Super-apostles" in 2 Corinthians 11:5 and 12:11 is also sarcastic.

[3]See my "Christ's Slave, People Pleasers and Galatians 1:10," *New Testament Studies* 42 (1996): 90-104, and "Paul's Paradigmatic 'I' and 1 Corinthians 6:12," *Journal for the Study of the New Testament* (forthcoming).

[4]For consideration of other charges about Paul's inconsistency, see Ernest Best, *Paul and His Converts* (Edinburgh: T & T Clark, 1988), pp. 146-50.

[5]Even the denial can be a way of making the point, a rhetorical technique called *antiphrasis.* That is, Paul may be shaming them and admonishing them! See Stephen M. Pogoloff, *Logos and Sophia: The Rhetorical Situation of 1 Corinthians,* Society of Biblical Literature Dissertation Series 134 (Atlanta: Scholars, 1992).

[6]Aristotle *The Art of Rhetoric* 2.6.12.

[7]Bruce J. Malina, *The New Testament World: Insights from Cultural Anthropology* (Atlanta: John Knox, 1981), pp. 25-50.

[8]E. R. Dodds, *The Greeks and the Irrational* (Berkeley: University of California Press, 1951), pp. 17-18.

[9]See Peter Marshall, "Invective: Paul and His Enemies in Corinth," in *Perspectives on Language and Text,* ed. Edgar W. Conrad and Edward G. Newing (Winona Lake, Ind.: Eisenbrauns, 1987), pp. 359-73.

[10]Nicholas Taylor, *Paul, Antioch and Jerusalem: A Study in Relationships and Authority in Earliest Christianity, Journal for the Study of the New Testament* Supplement 66 (Sheffield, England: JSOT, 1992), pp. 155-70, 227.

[11]Robert T. Fortna, "Philippians: Paul's Most Egocentric Letter," in *The Conversation Continues: Studies in Paul and John in Honor of J. Louis Martyn,* ed. Robert Fortna and Beverly Gaventa (Nashville: Abingdon, 1990), pp. 230.

[12]Gerald F. Hawthorne, *Philippians,* Word Biblical Commentary 43 (Waco, Tex.: Word, 1983), p. 3.

[13]See Peter T. O'Brien, "The Gospel and Godly Models in Philippians," in *Worship,*

Theology and Ministry in the Early Church: Essays in Honor of Ralph P. Martin, ed. Michael J. Wilkins and Terrence Paige, *Journal for the Study of the New Testament* Supplement 87 (Sheffield, England: JSOT, 1992), pp. 273-84.

[14]Gerhard Delling, *Paulus' Stellung zu Frau und Ehe* (Stüttgart: Kohlhammer, 1931), p. 144.

[15]An argument from silence is different from a case that is made by forming a hypothesis, testing that hypothesis and then stating the conclusion. It may be that reconstructions like this are a necessary element of historical interpretation, and the more evidence gathered the more a "maybe" becomes a "probably." This is different from stating a hypothesis as a fact with no collaborating evidence whatsoever.

[16]*Acts of Paul and Thecla* 3.

[17]Richard Bauckham, "Apocryphal Pauline Literature," in *Dictionary of Paul and His Letters,* ed. Gerald F. Hawthorne, Ralph P. Martin and Daniel G. Reid (Downers Grove, Ill.: InterVarsity Press, 1993), pp. 36.

[18]See Mary Stewart van Leeuwen, *Gender and Grace: Love, Work and Parenting in a Changing World* (Downers Grove, Ill.: InterVarsity Press, 1990), pp. 75-121.

[19]For a cautious and historically sensitive treatment of Pauline texts utilizing the psychological perspectives of learning theory, psychodynamics and cognition, see Gerd Theissen, *Psychological Aspects of Pauline Theology,* trans. John P. Galvin (1983; reprint Philadelphia: Fortress, 1987).

[20]This is the general scholarly consensus, but two recent articles argue that *thorn* is symbolic of people who reject Paul's apostolate (see Jerry W. McCant, "Paul's Thorn of Rejected Apostleship," *New Testament Studies* 34 [1988]: 550-72; Laurie Woods, "Opposition to a Man and His Message: Paul's 'Thorn in the Flesh' [2 Cor 12:7]," *Australian Biblical Review* 39 [1991]: 44-53). The list in 12:10 does not help settle this long-standing question, since it contains both physical calamities and personal opposition.

Chapter 8: Paul on His Best Day

[1]In a recent study, Brian Rapske (*The Book of Acts and Paul in Roman Custody,* vol. 3 of The Book of Acts in Its First Century Setting [Grand Rapids, Mich.: Eerdmans, 1994]) argues that one of the main purposes of Acts is to rehabilitate Paul's reputation, since his time in prison would have cast a negative social stigma on Paul. We may wonder whether this is one of Acts's main purposes, but Rapske alerts us to yet another problem that ancients would have had with Paul.

[2]Karl Barth, *Romans* (London: Oxford University Press, 1933), p. 1.

[3]Malcolm Muggeridge and Alec Vidler, *Paul, Envoy Extraordinary* (London: Collins, 1972), p. 13.